Inside Hillview High School

An Ethnography of an Urban Jamaican School

Hyacinth Evans

University of the West Indies Press
Jamaica • Barbados • Trinidad and Tobago
www.uwipress.com

University of the West Indies Press
7A Gibraltar Hall Road   Mona
Kingston 7   Jamaica
www.uwipress.com

10 09 08 07 06   5 4 3 2 1

CATALOGUING IN PUBLICATION DATA

Evans, Hyacinth L.
Inside Hillview High School: an ethnography of an urban Jamaican school /
Hyacinth L. Evans.

p. cm.
Includes bibliographical references.
ISBN: 976-640-194-2

1. Hillview High School (Jamaica). 2. Urban schools – Jamaica. 3. Education,
urban – Jamaica. 4. High school students – Jamaica – Attitudes. I. Title.

LC5143.J3E83 2006   370.097292

Book and cover design by Robert Kwak.

Set in Bodoni.

Printed in the United States of America.

Inside Hillview High School

For my daughter, Jessica

Contents

Acknowledgements

I wish to take this opportunity to express my appreciation to the many individuals who contributed to this study. My sincere thanks go to all the students of 9X without whom this research would not have been possible. Thank you for sharing with me your experiences, your joys, your doubts, your fears and your dreams.

I would like to express my gratitude to the principal of Hillview High School for granting me permission to carry out this study at his school. Mr Stewart gave me free access to all the school's facilities and resources. During the second year, I received similar consideration and support from the acting principal while the principal was on leave. Thanks, also, to all the teachers and guidance counsellors of Hillview High School for their friendliness and helpfulness during the almost two years of the study.

Finally, I would like to acknowledge the two anonymous reviewers who provided invaluable comments and suggestions that improved the quality of the original manuscript.

Thank you all.

Chapter 1   Setting the Stage

I see some idlers on the road and I wonder what
they are going to be in the future. I wouldn't like to
be like them. I wouldn't *be* like them, so that pushes
me a lot to do my work.

Sometimes, I think that if I don't do well, when
people get old, how are they going to live? So that's
why I have to do well from now so that I can take
care of my family.

The competition is hard. Everybody wants to go
further. Nobody not looking back.

– Grade 9 students on the need to achieve at school

This book is an examination of education, schooling, adolescent development
and academic achievement in one urban high school in Jamaica. The study
on which it is based grew out of my interest and concern about adolescents,
education, academic achievement and schooling. A primary reason for

conducting the study was the fact that most students in schools such as Hillview High School (all names in this report are pseudonyms) – a high school upgraded from a new secondary school – do not perform well on national tests such as those by the Caribbean Examinations Council (CXC) – a regional examination taken after five years of high schooling. What accounts for this level of performance? There is a great deal of evidence to show that the inequalities in students' chances of benefiting from the upper levels of education depend on social class background (Bowles and Gintis 1976; Karabel and Halsey 1977; Connell, Ashenden, Kessler and Dowsett 1982; Connell 1994). In nearly every country, educational outcomes such as performance on national examinations, retention rates in secondary schooling and access to higher education differ between social classes, geographical regions and ethnic groups. It is often asserted that such outcomes are a result of the differences in social capital (the knowledge, skills, attitudes and norms for behaviour that are valued by society) and cultural capital (the knowledge and concepts which form part of the family's background) that students bring to school and the socialization patterns that make middle-class students more capable of mastering the curriculum of schools.

However, as a teacher and teacher educator who visits schools regularly, I know that there are several factors, other than social and cultural capital, which have a major influence on students' learning and academic achievement. These include existential resources that individual students bring to the learning process: resources such as self-worth, self-regard, self-esteem, determination and self-affirmation, and a valuing of education. There are also factors within the school that affect academic performance. One can point to the teaching methods used in the school, the instructional materials available, the teacher-student relationship and the expectations that the school and the teachers hold for their students. In Jamaica, each of these elements may differ by type of school, though one can always find variations within a given type of school. CXC examination results consistently indicate that schools in Jamaica can be placed on a scale of performance, with one type of school – the upgraded high school – doing less well, on average, than the traditional and technical high schools.

In addition to my interest in finding explanations for students' levels of academic achievement, I also wanted to learn more about the ways in which students make sense of school and the means they employ to negotiate the multiple and often contradictory realities of home, school and community. This is of special interest in an age where the identity of students and the various ways of expressing that identity are increasingly contested, and where adolescents themselves have various sources of identity. The school is one of those sources and constitutes one of the most important sites for personality and identity formation. Another aim of the study was to disclose and challenge the role that schools play in our cultural life and in the lives of students. It is recognized that schooling plays an important role in the transition from childhood and adolescence to adulthood. As such, it has an enormous influence on the future of individual students and ultimately on the future of a society.

Perspectives on Academic Achievement

How have researchers and theorists explained the fact that, on average, students from poor, working-class or racially subordinated groups do not do as well academically as students from the middle classes or the racially dominant groups of society? Individual differences in achievement have been explained on the basis of differences in ability or intelligence or personal factors such as motivation. But how can group differences be explained? Much of the theorization about group differences in achievement has been done by educators in industrialized societies such as the United States, the United Kingdom and Australia and has been based on the experiences in these countries (for example, Connell 1994; Darling-Hammond 1995, 2000; Oakes 1985, 1995; Solomon 1992). Because it is mainly the poor and racially subordinated groups which do not achieve academically at school in these countries, much of the theorizing about the academic achievement and its causes focus on working-class and racially subordinated groups.

Mainstream psychology, which has traditionally studied factors affecting learning and academic achievement, has tended to de-emphasize or ignore characteristics of specific groups or sub-groups and the ways in which these characteristics and factors in the wider society influence individual academic outcomes. In Jamaica, we have learned from psychological research about the variables that correlate with secondary students' academic achievement. These studies used mainly causal comparative and correlational research designs and indicate that there is a strong relationship between students' academic ability and some cognitive and psychological characteristics such as spatial ability, abstract reasoning, field dependence, convergent thinking, self-conception of ability and academic achievement in various subjects (see studies reviewed in Evans 1997 and Hamilton 1991). Students' socio-economic status has also been shown to be strongly related to various academic outcomes (Hamilton 1991; Evans 1997). These studies focus on one or two independent variables with some form of academic outcome as the dependent variable. Research with a psychological orientation focuses on individual characteristics and generally ignores contextual factors.

Alternative explanations of student academic achievement pay attention to aspects of the social and cultural context – within the school or the society – that have an impact on student learning. Six of these alternative explanations are considered in this study. They are the social reproduction, the cultural reproduction, the cultural ecological, cultural production and social network theories, and considerations related to the cultural relevance of the curriculum and pedagogy. These theories are reviewed in appendix 2. Some of these explanations highlight the agency of the individual, for example, with respect to motivation and decision making, while some highlight the structure and processes of the school.[1] The school's social structures are actively constructed through the actions of individuals such as teachers and students. Processes such as teacher-student interaction can be the result of individual characteristics and sentiments and structures such as rules. In order to understand the outcomes of schooling, one has to gain information not only on students' inner perspectives, actions and behaviour, and the context in which these occur, but on the structures and processes that constrain, facilitate and influence teacher and student action. So the connection between structure and agency and the ways in which this connection gets played out in the school are of particular interest to a study concerned with the outcomes of schooling.

To make these connections between structure and agency, Mehan (1992) suggests a focus on "culturally constitutive action" on the part of individuals and the "constitutive rules" within institutions. In other words, Mehan is interested in the ways in which actions are constituted, how individuals interpret and react to institutional practices and requirements and the factors that influence their decisions and actions. In schools, institutional practices are the (constitutive) rules that shape students' lives and school career. To see the connection between structure and agency, there must be a focus on the meaning that individuals attribute to events, actions, symbols, structures and practices. In studying culturally constituted action, one examines the actions, decisions, judgements, choices, reactions and assessments that students and teachers make in response to institutional rules and practices. In examining educational outcomes, one is particularly interested in the constitutive practices that structure a student's learning, achievement and career choices.

Mehan's formulation fits with the interests, concerns and goals of the research reported here. As a researcher interested in how schools function, as well as in the meaning that students make of their experiences, I wanted to explore what lay behind these educational outcomes, which show that students in upgraded high schools have low levels of academic achievement, and the quantitative data of examination scores. How are the outcomes of schooling related to the school's rituals and practices, to pedagogical practices and other aspects of schooling? Furthermore, what are the salient features of the students' life world or their lived experiences that have an impact on the thinking and action of teachers and students? What are the mechanisms through and by which the status quo is reproduced in schools at this particular time in our history? In addition to the initial level of students' knowledge and academic achievement, what are learning, teaching, knowledge and knowledge acquisition like in these schools? These are the questions that animated this research to discover what teaching, learning and teacher-student interaction are like in an upgraded high school attended by mainly working-class students. I wanted to get students' views and perspectives on their experiences, to find out what sense they make of the curriculum, and how it connects with their lives and future aspirations. So in this study, there is a focus on school level and individual factors and the ways in which together they constitute and influence academic achievement.

As various school ethnographies have shown, qualitative research studies of schools and classrooms can provide specific data which help us understand the connection between social structure, school processes and students' academic achievement (Willis 1977; Ferguson 2000; Fine 1991; Anyon 1995; Dei et al. 1997). Some of these studies have shown that school structure and school processes marginalize certain students in many ways, and that schools do this according to race, class and gender. Ethnographic research can also help investigate the robustness of the explanations for educational achievement that have been shaped by experiences in other social contexts.

Framing the Study

Originally, I had an interest in studying the construction of subjective preferences during the adolescent years. This interest grew out of research I had carried out in Jamaica which showed that boys in the comprehensive high schools – as these upgraded high schools were then known – placed a lower value on education and believed that education would not prove to be very useful in later life (Evans 1998). These findings also showed that boys experienced conflicts with respect to studying and being studious, since this contradicted the prevailing masculine image. Similar results have been reported among Canadian Caribbean, African-American and Caribbean students in Britain (Fordham 1988; Solomon 1992; Sewell 1997). The school is an important site for identity formation or the formation of subjectivity. It is a place where personalities are formed or reinforced, and a place where knowledge about self and others is constructed. To this end, young people form friendship groups where they work toward the agenda of being accepted and validated: being a part of a group is significant.

These considerations framed the initial proposal for this study. I entered the school site with this notion of learning more about students' identities, gender differences in these identities, and the ways in which identities-in-formation influence academic achievement. However, as the research progressed, I became more interested in aspects of school life that could have an impact on academic achievement. It became clearer that students' subjectivities influence learning and achievement. And one's academic ability and achievement form an important aspect of one's identity. So these considerations regarding students' identity and subjective preferences, the challenges that they face at home and school and the ways in which the structure and processes of school influence their thinking and their subjectivity remained even as the study expanded to include learning and other outcomes.

The examination results which show that students in some schools perform poorly in national examinations make it clear that students in schools such as Hillview High School face many challenges in learning. The prevailing methods of teaching in Jamaican secondary schools, which I have documented in previous work (Evans 2001), may be a source of this difficulty. The transmission model of teaching, while very pervasive in secondary and tertiary institutions worldwide, is not conducive to the development of understanding. Connell (1994) has argued that this method of teaching, together with the curriculum, causes poor working-class children much difficulty in learning. Connell has linked this pedagogy to a particular curriculum which, in many cases, does not represent the experiences and perspectives of working-class students. Connell's argument suggests that the transmission model of teaching and the curriculum – which he terms the competitive academic curriculum – go hand in hand. For both reasons – the pedagogy and the curriculum – students will have difficulty learning.

In addition to the problem posed by the transmission model of teaching and a curriculum which rarely reflects or incorporates the experiences of working-class students, there is the issue of the relations between teachers and students. There is evidence that students – especially those from poor working-class families – suffer corporal punishment, verbal abuse and disrespectful treatment from some teachers on a continual basis. This type of teacher-student relationship, which forms the context for teaching and learning, may be one contributing factor to students' disengagement from learning experiences and from school and may in part explain the low academic achievement of these students.

The focus on academic achievement is justified on many grounds. High school students in Jamaica who do not do well at school or on national examinations rarely drop out of school, though many do leave school for various reasons such as financial difficulties. This is in contrast to what obtains in other countries such as the United States and the United Kingdom where a sizeable proportion of students from working-class and racially subordinated groups (as high as 55 per cent) disengage from and eventually drop out of school because of difficulties that have to do with learning, achievement, streaming and the nature of teacher-student interaction (Willis 1977; Rumberger 1987; Fine 1992; Dei et al. 1997). In Jamaica, students for the most part stay in school despite the academic and existential problems that schooling creates for them.[2]

There are consequences of low academic achievement for the individual, for the education system and for society. For example, students who do not do well on the CXC examination spend time and money repeating subjects. The Tracer study (1991–92) of students who had taken the CXC examination and had graduated from the various secondary schools showed that, among the students traced, more than one-third of those who continued their education repeated grade 11. The percentages of repeaters by type of school were: 32 per cent from the high school, 34 per cent from the new secondary school, 44 per cent from the technical school and 47 per cent from the comprehensive school (Brown 1994, 113). Furthermore, many students who did not succeed at the secondary level were obliged to continue their education in private secondary schools, the quality of which is still unknown. In addition to the time spent on repeating subjects and grades, failure can create uncertainty and frustration among students.

A high failure rate at the secondary level also has implications for access to the tertiary level and for the quality of personnel who enter the job market. In 2002, of the 19,400 persons who entered the job market, only 1,600 had five or more passes at the CXC level, 2,100 had less than five passes, while 12,500 passed no national examinations (STATIN 2002b). At the same time, in 2003, only 10.2 per cent of the cohort of secondary students gained access to the tertiary level of education (Ministry of Education, Youth and Culture 2003). In the Tracer study just cited, fewer students from the schools that were termed comprehensive and new

secondary schools (now the upgraded high schools) accessed tertiary education compared with those who attended the traditional high school. The
percentages of those who accessed tertiary education were 72 per cent for
the traditional high school compared with 48 per cent for the comprehensive
high school and 32 per cent for the new secondary school (Brown 1994).
Thus, when students do not achieve at the secondary level they are denied
access to tertiary education. This often results in a premature entry to the
job market for mainly unskilled work.

Academic achievement at the secondary level has enormous implications for the further education of the population and the quality of
the workforce. While the numbers gaining access to tertiary education
(including the teachers' colleges) have increased in recent years, access
to university education is still below the target set by the West Indian
Commission (West Indian Commission 1992). Low academic achievement
at the secondary level depresses the number of high school graduates and
the number of persons who can be prepared for mid-level technical and
administrative jobs in industry and commerce. A high school graduation
will be a requirement for most if not all jobs in Jamaica in the twenty-first
century. Furthermore, continued low achievement at the secondary level
lowers the society's confidence in the schools and the work of teachers.

In addition to the nation's work-related needs, academic achievement is critical to young peoples' sense of self and achievement.
Having a sense of efficacy is important for their future adaptation
in the wider society. Academic achievement and a sense of competence are not only a pivotal resource for positive identity development
during adolescence, they are the foundation on which the transition to
gainful employment is assured (Swanson, Spencer and Petersen 1998).
In a society which values academic achievement and in which such
achievement is recognized as the only basis for social advancement
and for individual status, academic failure can deal a harmful blow to
the adolescent's developing sense of self.

The school related factors in the upgraded high school which impact
achievement were of special interest. The research by Brown (1994) shows
that school effects can be more powerful than socio-economic status when it
comes to educational outcomes. In that study, it was found that "children from

less privileged social backgrounds who managed to gain access to the better secondary institutions (i.e. traditional high school) oftentimes outperformed their socially advantaged counterparts" (Brown 1994, 156). So if students in the upgraded high school do not do well academically, it is important to understand the school related factors that have an effect on these outcomes.

With this focus on academic achievement, there was an interest in determining the quality of teaching and learning at the secondary level, the support that students need and get in their pursuit of learning, and the extent to which classrooms are learning oriented. What is the process of learning like for these students? Do they have difficulty grasping concepts that may not be part of their experience? What supports do they need in learning and to what extent are these provided? The teacher-student relationship was included as an object of study since this is the basis for learning (Ennis and McCauley 2002; Erickson 1987) and is a critical factor in the theories of academic achievement which were reviewed.

The study assumes that students are not simply passive recipients of the knowledge that schools and teachers teach. They are not simply formed and moulded by the school. Students actively respond to requirements and pressures that they face and interrogate the messages and structures that make these demands on them. In the process of learning, they also develop attitudes to the subject, to the teachers and to the context. Some of these attitudes are developed and these interrogations are made in the company of or for the benefit of their peers. Peers play an important part in the development of the adolescent's preferences. So in examining the process of teaching and learning, it is necessary to pay attention to students' interactions with peers, especially the influential peers whose views and behaviours are admired. The values and beliefs gained from the peer network, as well as the nature of the peer relationship were included as a factor in the study. The peer relationship was seen as important as it is a site for negotiating the realities of school and home.

Constructing the Study

The study is an ethnographic case study of one class in an upgraded high school in urban Jamaica.[3] As Stake (2000, 435) explains, "case study is not a methodological choice but a choice of what is to be studied". In this case the object of study was an upgraded high school in urban Jamaica with a focus on one grade 9 class. The initial concerns and research interests have been outlined earlier. The research questions that guided the study were: How are the outcomes of schooling, particularly students' educational achievement, related to the rituals and school practices, pedagogical practices and to other aspects of schooling? What are the characteristics of learning, teaching, knowledge and knowledge acquisition that result in academic outcomes? What are the salient features of the students' life world that have an impact on the thinking and action of teachers and students? And how can the differences in academic outcomes by school or social group be explained? The main methods of data gathering used in this study were participant observation, interviewing, examination of site documents and a student questionnaire. I spent an entire academic year in the field collecting data and then returned the following year for another six months for additional interviews as these became necessary.

During the first term of the study, I visited the school roughly two times each week. The focus of observation initially was the classroom and the interactions that occurred therein. The interviewing of students and teachers took place during the second term. Six of the twelve subject teachers were interviewed on matters related to their teaching, their specialist subject, their views of teaching as a career and their views of grade 9X class. Members of class 9X were also interviewed in groups of three or four. The two guidance counsellors, the reading teacher and the vice-principal were also interviewed. In addition, I spoke with the principal on several occasions on matters related to students and teaching.

Much of the observation took place in room 9X but other aspects of students' behaviour were observed in other areas of the school, including the playing field, at special functions such as Boys' Day and meetings with the Parent-Teacher Association.[4] The 9X classroom is located off an open corridor and is bordered on two sides by two other grade 9 classrooms. The surrounding environment of room 9X was usually filled with activity and sounds of various sorts which could be heard from within 9X. Despite the fact that the room was well ventilated and the fan was always turned on, the classroom was usually hot. Added to this heat was the constant noise level caused by a variety of incidents including students' misbehaviour. The forty-two students in class 9X ranged in age from fourteen years to fifteen years and eight months at the start of the research. Almost one-half of these students lived with two parents or a parent figure and nearly one-third lived with their single mother. Most parents worked at skilled or semi-skilled jobs, though a few were professionals. Most parents lived in inner city areas of Kingston. Further information on the methodology and research design, including the process of gaining entry to the field, field relations, the use of key informants, ensuring validity and guarding against bias, the process of interpretation, and preserving ethics and confidentiality are provided in appendix 1.

Reflections on the Researcher's Role

Unlike other research methodologies, the primary instrument of data collection in qualitative research is the researcher. It is, therefore, important to recognize my own subjectivity in carrying out this research. I have already outlined the main interests that influenced my desire to do this study – in particular my concern with students' academic achievement and development in the upgraded high school. The framing of the study was also influenced by my views on the nature of learning which is constructed and influenced by the context in which it takes place. I have also been influenced by the critical/cultural studies approach to education and its focus on uncovering inequities, domination and oppression in the system. All these orientations influenced the study. I was, in some respects, privileged to be able to enter the school to carry out this study – being a member of the University of the West Indies and a researcher in education. I was mindful of this privilege and wished to use it to create a better understanding of students' lives in schools and their efforts to learn and achieve.

There were of course major differences between myself and the students whom I was studying, namely differences in age and status. So I had to examine myself and reflect on the connections between myself and the students I was studying. What did I have in common with these grade 9 students? How could I create common ground so that I could come to understand their lives and experiences? This forced me to think of who

I was and what I brought to the research process and to the relationship with the students. There were in fact few defining aspects of my identity that would make for common bonds between me and the students in 9X. They were adolescent students, male and female, from mainly working-class families. These children had a reputation of being noisy and at times disruptive. I saw myself as a somewhat studious, middle-class adult who grew up in the country, but who was now an urban woman, and a university professor. What connected me most of all with the students was my rural upbringing, my familiarity with poor working-class people whom I had known as a child, and the fact that I had experienced an early schooling which, in some respects, was similar to theirs.

Although I was familiar with traditional high schools in Jamaica, having attended one, having taught in another, and having entered many as a teacher educator and researcher, I soon realized that Hillview High School reminded me not of traditional high schools but of the elementary school that I had attended in the 1950s and 1960s. In rural areas, the elementary school, now called the all age school, was the school for everyone except the very few who attended private schools in the city. I went to an elementary school attended by children of farmers, teachers, the minister of religion, policemen, maids (as they were then called) and businesspersons. Because it was a rural school, most children came from poor backgrounds, as did the students in this study. As Metz (1993) and others have observed, it is the students, their behaviour, actions and general comportment that primarily make up the culture of a school. And, on reflection, I concluded that the student body had a lot to do with the look and feel of Hillview High School. In some respects, it was the culture of this school and its similarity to my elementary school that created, in my mind, a commonality. As a researcher, however, I came to this culture of schooling with specific research questions and perspectives which shaped the data collected and the interpretive frames used to analyse this data.

The class that became the focus of this study was chosen by the school. It had some characteristics which, as it turned out, also provided useful information on the construction of academic achievement. The school in which the study was conducted practised streaming. The choice of this class provided an opportunity to study, in-depth, a streamed class in which students were of mixed ability. The class itself was not a high stream class, being fourth in the informal system of ranking of streamed classes. This combination of mixed ability and streaming provided further insights into the many ways in which academic achievement is constructed. Thus, the study is about a grade 9 class of mixed ability operating in a streamed system and in which students are not high achievers. It is located in an upgraded high school where resources are limited and the parents and community are unable to provide the additional resources to support the school. In these respects, this high school and this class are representative of roughly one-half of all high school classrooms in Jamaica today. According to the *Survey of Living Conditions* (STATIN 1998), students from the poorest consumption groups are overrepresented in the upgraded schools (formerly the comprehensive and new secondary schools). Data obtained from the Ministry of Education, Youth and Culture show that the facilities and resources in roughly one-half of these upgraded schools are either weak or average. These percentages vary by region.

The Case Study: Its Limits and Possibilities

The case study focuses on one entity which has some "boundedness". In the human and social sciences, the "case has working parts; it is purposive; it often has a self; it is an integrated system" (Stake 2000, 436). The researcher assumes that there are regularities and patterns of behaviour in a case that can shed light on a wider phenomenon or the class which that case represents. The case study allows for an in-depth study of these patterns of behaviour and internal processes. The researcher examines all aspects of this case – in this instance, an institution – that has bearing on the research questions, choosing the most appropriate data gathering methods to obtain the information desired. Through this in-depth study and the detailed understanding that develops, one gains insight not only into these internal processes and patterned behaviour, but an understanding of the wider phenomenon or class that the case represents.

In choosing a case, therefore, one has to ask what is this a case of? What phenomenon or class does it represent? In this instance, the case was an institution and the class of institution that it represented was the upgraded high school in Jamaica. I studied this particular school in order to understand a wider phenomenon – upgraded high schools – and to answer research questions related to students' academic achievement and development. What can a particular case tell us about the larger group and the wider phenomenon? How, in other words, can one generalize from a particular case? The advantage of the case study is the study of the particular, namely, the details of the processes, the decisions, the relationships, the rules, the curriculum, the methods of teaching and the ways in which these are interrelated. In describing what occurs at Hillview High School and, in particular, in class 9X, I am interested in presenting the particulars of that institution and that class. I want my readers to become interested in, perhaps to care about Hillview High School, the students of 9X and what happens in that institution. But, I would also like them to develop some understanding of what upgraded high schools are like and how the phenomenon in question – students' academic achievement – is constructed in upgraded high schools. In other words, I would like readers to be able to see connections and similarities between Hillview High and other upgraded high schools, and to develop an understanding of the important and complex issue of the construction of academic achievement in high schools. In the words of Stake (2000, 439), "the search for particularity competes with the search for generalizability", but both can be achieved.

In a qualitative case study, generalization is not based on appropriate sampling procedures and statistical methods, as is done in statistically based research designs. Rather, the process is based on comparison between the case in question or specific aspects of the case and other instances of the larger group. The reader recognizes specific instances or situations and determines whether there is a basis for comparison or comparability. This type of generalization has been termed "naturalistic generalization", and is done by the reader or consumer of the research rather than by the researcher. "In their experiential and contextual accounts, case study researchers assist readers in the construction of knowledge" (Stake 2000, 443). The researcher, however, tries to facilitate this process of generalization through many design decisions and through the conduct of the research itself. The first decision has to do with the typicality of the case chosen. In this case, Hillview High School is fairly typical of urban upgraded high schools with respect to its size, staff and student population, the curriculum, and the financial, material, pedagogical and behavioural issues that it faces. But generalization depends on more than typicality of the case. The reader has to make comparisons and recognize similarities. In order to help the reader in this process of recognition and comparison, the researcher describes the case in sufficient detail (what is referred to as thick description) and, in addition, pays attention to the general variables that are of wider interest – the curriculum, the teaching, the interactions, the examinations, the rituals and rules and the various situations that occur in schools. The reader must also develop confidence in the credibility and trustworthiness of the data. The procedures which I followed in order to ensure credibility and trustworthiness are outlined in the research methodology and the research design described in appendix 1.

This case study is also an ethnography and can be compared with several other ethnographic accounts of schooling. As Hammersley and Atkinson have pointed out, an ethnography "involves the ethnographer participating, overtly or covertly, in people's daily lives for an extended period of time, watching what happens, listening to what is said, asking questions – in fact collecting whatever data are available to throw light on the issues that are the focus of the research" (1993, 1). This description reflects the processes followed in this research. The study falls within the tradition of critical ethnography which goes beyond the portrayal and disclosure of what exists and the description of the meaning perspectives of participants. Meaning perspectives refer to the meanings that individuals ascribe to events and which are influenced by the unique perspective that those individuals hold. Critical ethnography seeks to examine the structures of domination in institutions and society that place constraints on individual lives, in order to expose power relations and the causes of inequality.

The next chapter outlines some of the issues and perspectives that have a bearing on the issues identified and on students' learning outcomes.

Notes

1. Within the school setting, we can regard structures as the specific rules, institutional practices, resources or policies that are part of the institution which serve to influence behaviour and action. According to Connell (1987, 92), "the concept of social structure expresses the constraints that lie in a given form of social organization. . . . It reflects the experience of being up against something, of limits on freedom." Despite this binary of agency and structure, each influences the other. Individual action may often influence structure, and elements of structure, such as the policy of streaming in a school, can influence the thinking and behaviour of individuals, and may shape his or her thought and action (Giddens 1979, 5).

2. Very few Jamaican students drop out of school voluntarily. Bearing in mind that a student may voluntarily drop out of school for a variety of reasons including migration and transfers to other schools, the drop-out rates cited by Education Statistics for 2002–3 ranged from 0.4 per cent (grades 3 to 4) to 3.6 per cent (grades 5 to 6). Education Statistics does not publish drop-out rates for grades 9 to 11 because it is difficult to make this calculation. "Promotion and drop-out rates from grades 9–10 and grades 11–12 cannot be calculated as most students in All Age and Primary and Junior High Schools complete the secondary level at grade 9." These students (roughly eight thousand each year) drop out of school each year because there are no facilities for them. Because of the number of secondary places available at the grade 10 level, many students of the all-age school leave grade 9 with no place available for them. This structure with limited access to grade 10 for many poor students is a holdover from all-age schools of the pre-independence days when these schools prepared the literate working class who were expected to enter domestic and agricultural service at age fifteen years. (My thanks to an anonymous reviewer for this information on the all-age school of the pre-independence era.)

3. Stake (2000) describes three types of case studies: the intrinsic, in which the researcher and the reader are interested in the particular case because of its intrinsic interest and peculiarities; the instrumental case study which is examined mainly to provide insight into an issue; and the collective case study in which the researcher studies a number of cases. Based on this description, this study can be described as an instrumental case study. However, Stake acknowledges that one can read an instrumental case study and have an intrinsic interest in it, and at the same time learn about the class that it represents.

4. In recent years, many schools have instituted special events or activities such as Boys' Day to address the problem of the level of academic achievement of boys which, on average, is less than that of girls. The nature of the event or

activity varies. In the case of Boys' Day at Hillview High, a special effort was made to address the concerns of boys and to invite fathers to school so that they could all discuss issues with the boys. Entertainers with a "message" meaningful to boys also performed on this day. Girls did not come to school on that day. There was no equivalent Girls' Day during the time of the research.

Chapter 2 Issues and Perspectives

This chapter provides some background to the issues that framed the study, including the role and function of the secondary school in Jamaican society, the context for adolescent development in Jamaica, and colour and class in Jamaica.

The School in Jamaican Society

The school in Jamaica, like schools everywhere, offers the promise of opportunities, the benefits of the knowledge and skills that undergird the modern state and provide certification for entry to occupations and a better life. Schools have been established to encourage and facilitate the mastery of knowledge and disciplines that have currency and applications in wider spheres (Levinsom, Foley and Holland 1996). The mastery of these knowledges, disciplines and skills has become more and more critical to young people everywhere, as societies become modern. The promise of such opportunities has been particularly significant to post-colonial societies. Jamaica, for instance, was founded on inequality, with whites exercising control and dominance over blacks in almost every respect, and with blacks for many years being denied the benefits of the most basic of human rights and dignities, including education.

From the very beginnings of mass education in Jamaica, the Jamaican people have participated in education whenever they were able to do so. Immediately after emancipation, the freed slaves gave large subscriptions for educational purposes to the various religious bodies (Great Britain Board of Education 1901). At that time, the religious bodies reported a significant increase in enrolment as parents and children "looked to education as a means of obtaining political privileges and advancement in life" (King 1998, 47). This participation in education has continued to the present day where there is almost 100 per cent enrolment in primary and secondary education to grade 9 level. This high level of participation has continued despite the fact that the state has not provided quality education for the mass of Jamaicans (Miller 1989, 208). Though students and parents have responded to the call to education by their presence and their participation, they have not all received the benefits and outcomes expected of the school in the modern state: outcomes such as a certificate that would qualify them for employment. The disparity in outcomes can be attributed, in part, to the many inequalities in the system.

King (1998) has argued that the roots of educational inequality lie deeply buried in the colonial past. The school was created to serve certain interests to preserve the status quo and to maintain the inequalities that characterized a colonial society. Thus, in accordance with the racial thinking of the day, a dual system of education was established – one for whites and one for blacks. The high school, established toward the end of the eighteenth century, was meant for the rising middle classes, the whites and browns; was intended to serve the interests of those in power; and was intended to maintain a social and educational distance between them and the black masses (King 1999). The elementary school, later termed the all-age school, was established soon after emancipation for the education of the black masses. However, it was meant mainly to socialize students to their secondary status in the society and to give them the rudimentary skills of reading and writing. In this way, the status quo would be maintained. A society that was racially, socially and economically divided and in which privileges were accorded to whites was preserved. Some among the ruling white elite did not even think that education was suited for blacks. Others felt that the school should play the important role of "training children in habits of discipline and subordination" (Bryan 2000b, 116–17; Turner 1987). The upper grades of the elementary school, grades 7 to 9, provided the only secondary education available to most black children for most of the nineteenth century and a major part of the twentieth century. The curriculum offered by this school was, however, merely an extension of the primary curriculum and was not the equivalent of a grade 7 to 9 high school education. The curriculum for grades 7 to 9 of the elementary/all-age school remained in effect until the 1990s when the ROSE curriculum was introduced.[1] Thus, a stratified educational system was established to match the racially and socially stratified society that existed and which, in fact, still exists.

New secondary schools were first established in the 1960s in order to increase access to the secondary level. At that time, approximately 6 per cent of primary-school graduates had access to the high schools which were the only secondary schools at that time. However, the creation of a new type of secondary school – the new secondary school – continued the dual system of education whereby there were different educational paths, each with different entry requirements, curricula and examinations. The basis for admission to the high schools remained selective with the Common Entrance Examination, but admission to these new secondary schools was non-selective. In other words, students did not have to pass an entrance examination to enter the new secondary schools. There was "free flow" admission to these schools. The starting points of these two systems were quite different.

There were differences in the curriculum and the examinations offered by the high schools and the new secondary schools. The new secondary schools offered a curriculum that culminated in the Jamaica School Certificate, later the Secondary School Certificate, which became a requirement for entry to certain occupations. Since performance on the Common Entrance Examination was highly correlated with social class (Gordon 1991), students who attended these two types of secondary schools differed in their social class origins. Most students who attended the high schools came from the middle and upper classes, while most students who attended the new secondary schools were from a lower socio-economic background. So a distinction continued to be made in the minds of Jamaicans between the high schools that had been established for the middle and upper classes and these new secondary schools.

Although there was an expansion of secondary-level schools, the dual system of education with different curricula, different examinations, different expectations for the racially different students and different funding arrangements continued. There were two separate paths for getting an education: the prep school/high school path and the elementary/all-age school/new secondary school/teachers' college path. These two paths represented "the social cleavages and discontinuities of the society" (Miller 1989). They represented the two Jamaicas separated by race, colour and economic and political power. This dual system of education and the social cleavages it represented have contributed to a lack of unity in the society (Sherlock and Bennett 1998). Some have argued that this dual system of education has also served to perpetuate the state of Jamaica's class relations, for "the inferior education offered the working class has acted as a sieve blocking their passage out of manual labour" (Austin 1984, xiii).[2]

This dual system has been modified somewhat in recent years as there is some integration between the two paths. Primary education is now integrated with secondary education and the majority of those admitted to secondary schools and to the high schools are graduates of primary schools. Entry to teachers' colleges is now based on successful completion of high school and graduates of the teachers' colleges matriculate to the university. However, as Miller (1989) points out, the dual system has not been completely eliminated. It is true that the majority of those who are admitted to the high schools are now graduates of the primary schools, unlike the situation that existed in the 1950s when the majority of those admitted to high schools came from the prep (private fee-paying) schools. Nevertheless, roughly 30 per cent of the graduates of primary schools do not get places in the high schools, which now include the upgraded high schools.[3] In these and other respects, inequality in education continues.

Another important contributor to the dual system was the curriculum which, until recently, differed by type of school. Up to the 1970s, the curriculum of the high school was based on overseas examination syllabuses such as the General Certificate of Education (GCE) O and A levels. After 1972, when the Caribbean Examinations Council was established, the CXC and Caribbean Advanced Proficiency (CAPE) examinations replaced the GCE O- and A-level examinations for most subjects in most high schools. High school students were prepared to pass these examinations which assured entry to universities and to white-collar jobs. The curriculum of the other schools was locally developed, was not valued by employers and did not ensure entry to universities. The introduction of the ROSE curriculum for grades 7 to 9 in the 1990s was the start of the integration of the secondary school system. By the 1990s, all schools were required to offer the ROSE programme to grade 9, after which students were prepared for the regional CXC examination. However, many of the upgraded high schools, which have only recently begun to offer the CXC programme, have experienced some difficulty in preparing all their students for this examination. For varying reasons, some students in these schools are not entered for any examination. These are other indicators of the inequality in educational opportunity.

Reflections on the Secondary-Education System

Olive Senior has referred to the paradox of the education system in Jamaica: on the one hand, many graduates of this country's secondary schools record great achievements at home, in the Caribbean and the rest of the world, whereas, on the other hand, a significant portion of graduates do not. She says, "while some students continue to do well, especially those privileged to attend the so-called elite schools, education for the masses of children is still second-rate or beyond their means" (2003, 171). Here, Senior speaks directly to the result of the dual system of education established centuries ago, which continues to exercise its influence today.

Despite its many achievements, the education system is seen by some as a system that alienated students from their culture, history and nation, mainly as a result of the curriculum, which was, for most of its history, not designed for Jamaicans and for nation building. This colonial education, which inculcated colonial attitudes and values, in many ways reinforced the messages of the wider society and alienated young people from their own history, culture and ancestors. "The goals, values, methods, outlook of Jamaica's system of education remained colonial and generated split loyalties. . . . [It was] . . . the chief barrier to social development" in the 1950s (Sherlock and Bennett 1998, 387). There are others who argue that this curriculum focused on Britain, its culture and values did not allow for a knowledge and understanding of other cultures, issues and events – in particular those having to do with the African diaspora, its peoples and cultures.

So, while the education of the traditional high school has provided an entry to wider opportunities, it has also been criticized for its lack of focus on the development of the individual, especially with respect to self-esteem and self-confidence. This self-confidence has been difficult to achieve because of the failure to acknowledge the inner world of a people whose ancestors had experienced slavery and to recognize that the values of the colonizers had been internalized throughout the long dark years of slavery and the years after emancipation. The young are constantly bombarded with messages of white superiority at every turn – in images of beauty, in valuations of our culture, in colonial and racial stereotypes, among others. In the post-colonial era, it was not seen as necessary for the education system to address the issue of self-esteem – a necessary condition for developing self-confidence as individuals and as a people. This absence of attention to the social and emotional aspects of adolescent development continues to this day, with the criteria for evaluating high schools placed mainly, if not solely, on academic achievement.

There has been increasing criticism of high schools in Jamaica since the upgrading of about 75 comprehensive or new secondary schools to high school status in 1999. In these public evaluations of schools, the focus has been on the academic achievement of students and the ranking of schools with respect to their performance in national and regional examinations such as the CXC examination. Critics often compare the performance of Jamaican schools with other Caribbean countries (Thompson 2003; Chuck 2004). They also cite the difference in academic achievement between the traditional high schools and the upgraded high schools. Although traditional and upgraded high schools vary in quality and the academic achievement of their students, upgraded high schools do, on average, perform less well than the traditional high schools. The results of the regional CXC examinations show that, on average, a higher percentage of students in traditional high schools gain passes in both Mathematics and English.[4] So when the upgraded high school is compared with the traditional high school, the problem of academic achievement becomes quite evident. One reason for undertaking this study was my desire to find solutions to this achievement gap. However, many of those who criticize upgraded high schools and the work that they do often do not take into account the enormity of the task of improving schools that were established as separate and unequal from the very start. These upgraded schools are faced with the challenge of overcoming the burden of inferior status, and critics often fail to realize that the two types of schools were established at different periods and have different histories and legacies which continue to exercise an influence on what happens in these institutions. The upgrading of the new secondary schools to high school status is only one of the actions taken over the past thirty or so years to integrate the dual system and to create equality of educational opportunity among schools that are at different starting points. Public criticism of schools, and in particular, of the upgraded high schools shows the emphasis on academic achievement and performance on national examinations almost to the exclusion of other ends of education. Rarely is mention made of the social emotional development of students, the development of character identity and self-confidence and willingness to contribute to one's community. The criteria for evaluating our schools are limited in part because education has always played such a key role in advancing social mobility. The society has always placed such great faith in education as a means of social and economic advancement that it rarely takes the time to consider these other important ends of education, ends which would speak to other criteria for judging schools.

Education and Schooling

Jamaican high schools display the universal features of schools. The buildings are usually built in the same fashion with the familiar egg-crate design, and with halls and walkways constructed off rows of classrooms that look alike. The rooms are usually of the same size designed for about thirty but often accommodating about forty, fifty or sixty students. There are varying kinds of chairs and desks facing a blackboard near which is the teacher's table. The physical appearance of the buildings is more or less the same, though some schools may obviously need a new coat of paint, and some may have panes of windows missing. The lawns and gardens may be more poorly kept in some schools than in others. School is in session about seven to eight hours a day except in cases where the school is on the shift system. Teachers teach one or two subjects and have an average of four to five sessions per day. The high schools offer subjects in a curriculum that is defined by the CXC, CAPE or GCE syllabuses, and these syllabuses and textbooks define what is taught.

What distinguishes one school from another are not so much these features but the culture of the school, the rituals and routines, the meanings that students, teachers and other adults accord to them, the relationships established among teachers and between teachers and students, the priorities placed on certain values, and the expectations held for students. Some argue that the characteristics of students also make a big difference to the culture of a high school (Metz 1993). Despite the official rhetoric of equality among schools (the existence of a centralized curriculum is usually used to justify this claim), there are cultural differences in schools, differences in the pedagogical processes and the content and tone of classroom discourse that make a difference in the lives of students as well as in educational outcomes. Each high school occupies a different location in relation to the wider society and makes a different contribution to the life trajectories of its students.

Although the school is a distinct institution with its walls and fences, education is never a closed system. As Connell (1993) states, "schools are interwoven with their milieux". Families and the communities of the students have a major influence on the culture and functioning of the school. Depending on their social location, parents can be a vibrant part of the school, shaping its policies, culture and resources, or they can be passive or non-participant. It is true that conducting relationships with schools requires various resources on the part of the parent, and cultural capital is certainly one of these. Depending on the socio-cultural match between the teachers and the school, the relationship between the parents and the school can be smooth or abrasive and frustrating. Parent-school relationships form part of the contextual resources of a school which also include the financial resources at the community's disposal. The inequalities in the contextual resources for schools in part define the historical situation in which a school or an educational system finds itself (Connell 1993). Parents and the public recognize that schools are unequal, although they may not always take into account the differences in the resources available to each school. Evidence of the public's recognition of the inequality among schools is seen in the school choices parents make for their children when they apply to sit the Grade Six Achievement Test (GSAT). In this instance, the traditional high schools are usually the first choice and parents hope that their children will receive high enough scores to be placed in these schools. This occurs every year when primary and prep school students sit the GSAT.[5]

Accounts of schooling in Jamaica underscore the fact that schools and teachers treat students differentially according to their socio-economic status, race, class or gender (Phillips 1973; Keith 1976; Sistren 1986; Evans 2001). Similar research results have been reported for other countries such as the United States and Canada (McLaren 1989; Giroux 1996; Dei et al. 1997). Ascribable characteristics such as good manners, behaviour and language have an impact on this treatment, as do student qualities such as respectfulness, docility and even obedience. These behaviours often underlie the rules and routines of the school, especially the high school. Middle-class students usually come to school not only possessing the cultural capital of their parents, but the behaviours that schools value and expect. They are able to display the latter with relative ease. Middle-class students are therefore well positioned to interact positively with teachers and to follow the rules and routines of the school. Their cultural knowledge, which consists of the manners, behaviour and decorum that they bring to school, also helps to make them ideal students. Many students who come from poor working-class families and who live in communities rife with violence, conflict, frustration and stress often find it difficult to behave appropriately in schools. For some, their experiences have produced accustomed behaviours that are not usually sanctioned by the school. In this way, schools and classrooms usually enhance the success of those who have been raised in the most favoured environment. However, autobiographies of eminent Jamaicans and other Caribbean nationals indicate that schools have played a significant role in the lives of many working-class students and have contributed significantly to their upward social mobility despite the difficulties that they experienced (James 1963; Clarke 1980; Thompson 2000).

Working-class students come to school usually speaking a language that has little status in the society, and do not easily or willingly conform to the school's image of the ideal student. Even when they possess the cultural capital that will put them in good stead as students, they may not have the consensually validated norms that are so important to the school. There are some who are inclined to learn these behaviours and to become the type of student that the school desires. Today, however, there are many students who are not inclined to learn behaviours that represent something different from their lived experiences. This has been shown to be the case in many schools in the United States, Canada and the United Kingdom where working-class youth, especially males, are unwilling to adopt the behaviours that high schools expect of students. This causes a conflict between teachers and students because these students are far more willing to question the authority of the school and to show lack of interest in and even disdain for the school's curriculum and pedagogy. Despite these changes in the perspectives of young people, schools have not easily adjusted their teaching approaches to accommodate the lived experiences and perspectives of youth (Giroux 1996; McLaren 1989). Kelly's (2003) research suggests that, in Jamaica, some teachers are not willing to make these adjustments.

Adolescence in the Jamaican Context

The students in this study ranged in age from fourteen years to fifteen years and eight months at the start of the investigation. By the usual age-related criteria, they are in early or middle adolescence. Adolescence is regarded as a period of transition from childhood to adulthood – a period when biological, emotional and social processes as well as societal demands create changes in the individual and in his or her social status. The young people in this study, however, occupy a rather contradictory position with respect to their status in the home and society and their place in the life cycle. Many of them have already been initiated into adulthood or adult ways of life. They have assumed adult roles at the same time that they attend school and perform the role of student and child, as Jamaican researcher Claudette Crawford-Brown (1999) has shown. These students form part of that group referred to as "youth", who are below the age of twenty-five. Those aged fifteen to twenty-four years made up roughly 18 per cent of the Jamaican population while those in the thirteen to fifteen age group made up approximately 6 per cent of the population in 2002 (STATIN 2002a). The fact that these young people are from the working-class group in the society makes them very typical of Jamaican youth.

The notion of a period of moratorium between childhood and the assumption of adult responsibilities gradually took hold in Western societies around the turn of the twentieth century when schooling became compulsory. In contrast, in Jamaica and the rest of the Carib-bean, the experience of slavery eliminated childhood and adolescence as periods in the life cycle for the vast majority of the population. For much of Jamaica's history, young people who graduated from the elementary school (now called the all-age school) did so at age fourteen or fifteen and had few options but to try to find some type of job – usually domestic or farm labour. Further education was virtually impossible for the vast majority of young people. It is only in the last two generations or so that the period of adolescence has been acknowledged as a distinct period in a person's life, and secondary schooling has become increas-ingly accessible to more young people as more of these institutions were constructed. Increased access to education thus allowed them to delay work or pregnancy (Barrow 2001, xxiii).

Today, this period of adolescence is acknowledged as a distinct and important period in the development of Jamaican youth. Teachers and counsellors in training are taught the characteristics of the adolescent and the tasks and challenges that young people face at this time of their lives. The views of psychologists, sociologists and anthropologists regarding adolescence have been adopted in some circles in the Jamaican society, though these views have not been embraced by all. There are many in the society, including the parents and teachers of adolescents, who have different views of adolescents' rights and responsibilities and the way in which they should be treated. Some parents (and teachers) believe in the adage "Children should be seen and not heard", and dispense corporal punishment at the slightest infraction. Others recognize that adolescents need much guidance and should be gradually introduced to adult-like responsibilities. These differing views stem in part from different cultural traditions and different views of the status and rights of children who are dependent on adults, even as parents and teachers exercise authority over them. It is not surprising that Phillips found in his study of adolescence in Jamaica that, "between classes, the difference[s] are so great as almost to constitute different sub-cultures" (1973, v).

For this period of transition to be given true meaning, the economic and social circumstances must exist for the adults, parents or parental figures to provide the social, emotional and physical space for young people to experience it. In poor, working-class groups this is not usually the case, as economic circumstances often require adolescents to assume housekeeping and child-rearing roles or even engage in income generating activities. Parents may lack knowledge about adolescent development and the kinds of experiences that could aid in the young person's overall development. They may simply lack the wherewithal to provide these experiences. We have limited information on how these circumstances affect the adolescent at school. For example, Phillips (1973) found that the academic work and attendance of many secondary students suffered because they had to assume domestic or farm chores. We have little information on the extent to which the school helps adolescents to manage and understand their experiences at home by providing the guidance, support and encouragement that will help them through these turbulent years.

In most countries, society's response to adolescents' behaviour differs by gender, race and class. However, much of the literature on adolescence does not deal with differences by race and class (Griffin 1993) and does not always acknowledge that society's response to adolescents' behaviour differs by gender, race and class. Young adolescents from a working-class background are often not granted any special consideration when they engage in inappropriate behaviours (Giroux 1996).

Adolescence is a particularly significant phase of life during which young people try to figure out who they are. Their sense of self (their identity, real or imagined) is an important motivating force in life. It is developed through their lived experiences and through interactions with significant others such as parents, friends, siblings and teachers. Adolescents pay attention to their own as well as others' responses to their behaviour. They use social comparison to evaluate themselves. This, however, can be confusing since there are so many reference groups with which they would like to identify. Parents, friends and peers may have an important influence on them, but so too may media personalities and others who have the material possessions or qualities that are admired by the society. Because adolescents are going through a developmental process and are trying on various identities, the self at this stage may fluctuate and be contradictory. Appropriate experiences that are consistent and developmental will help adolescents to integrate these aspects of the self and lead to better self-understanding (Phillips 1973; Swanson, Spencer and Petersen 1998; Newman 1998; Schaps, Battistich and Solomon 1997).

Theories of adolescence and adolescent development reflect different orientations. One theory is the ecological theory, such as that of Bronfenbrenner (1995), which takes into account the various contexts in which the individual is located. This theory states that one's behaviour is ecologically nested and it highlights the adolescent as an active agent in a series of interrelated systems. The environmental context, from the micro (home setting) to the macro levels (social and cultural contexts), provides relevant experiences that interact with psychological processes to produce behaviour (Swanson, Spencer and Petersen 1998). The ecological perspective is reflected in the framework developed by the World Bank in its review of the factors that have an impact on youth in the Caribbean. The authors of the report see human development and youth development taking place in overlapping interrelated spheres that include home, family, school and community (World Bank 2003, 9). Their framework includes macro-environmental factors such as the mass media (radio, television, videos, movies, newspapers and magazines), the state of the national economy, the nature of public institutions, the cultural and historical background, and cultural values related to gender. Micro-environmental factors refer to the institutions such as the family and the school, communities and social networks which are all important in providing material care, support, comfort, guidance and avenues for experimentation and validation.

Theories such as the ecological theory of development assume that the institutions in the immediate environment such as the home and the school will act in a caring and supportive manner in order to ensure the adolescent's well being and proper development: adults will act benevolently and be proper role models; parents will provide love, care, material support, guidance and protection at all times; the home will be the place where there is harmony, and cohesiveness and a stable and safe environment will be created; teachers will pass on the essentials of the culture in a benevolent and caring manner to all and their authority will be used in a benign manner for the proper development of the young; and the church will provide experiences for the development of their spirituality. Such assumptions reflect the structural-functionalist view of society where institutions and individuals in authority are supposed to embody what is good for society. The reality in Jamaica and in many other parts of the world is often quite different, for dysfunctions occur in many of these institutions, including the family and the school, which do not always cater to the proper development of children and adolescents.

The Jamaican Family and Adolescent Development

The Western view of the family as the agent of socialization for young people often assumes the existence of the nuclear family, but such a family structure exists for only a small minority of families worldwide, even within the developed world. As Barrow points out, "the majority of the world's children have never known and will not experience life within a nuclear family, based on marriage and co-residence. . . . Indeed very few families of the region conform to the bourgeois ideals of marriage, nuclear domestic groups and patriarchal household headship" (2001, xxix). The view of the "normal" family and normative family structure also exercises its influence in Jamaica and other parts of the Caribbean despite the fact that the majority of Jamaican families do not conform to this pattern. Family life in Jamaica and other countries of the Caribbean is character-ized by extra-residential or visiting relationships, common law unions, female household headship and three generational family homes (Barrow 2001, xxix). In Jamaica, 58 per cent of children did not have fathers resid-ing with them (Roopnarine 2004) and 45.5 per cent of households were headed by females in 2002 (STATIN 2002b). Because of the prevalence of visiting and non-residential unions, children are often cared for by numer-ous adults in extended family units. But in an alarming number of cases, children (mostly from working-class groups) are left by migrating parents with no systematic source of support (Crawford-Brown 1999).

Among working-class families, child-rearing practices lean toward harsher forms of discipline that are situated in more autocratic parenting styles and, so, are less likely to support intellectual curiosity. A practice that works in tandem with these beliefs is the enforcement of physical punishment to bring children in line with adults' ideas about behavioural conduct. The prevalence and tolerance of corporal punishment is well documented. Its prevalence goes back to the days of slavery when "the school system was based on terror", the beatings at home complemented the flogging meted out by the teacher, and the father's authority often rested on fear (Bryan 2000b, 120). Furthermore, at that time, the consequences of violating conventions were usually so harsh and swift that parents felt compelled to make their children learn by force in order to avoid facing these consequences. This authoritarian type of discipline contrasts with the parenting style of middle- and upper-class Jamaicans. Recent studies reveal that almost 60 per cent of these parents use authoritative parenting styles instead, whereby there is an equal emphasis on support, nurturing and love as there is on pressure to conform (Ramkisoon 2002 reported in Roopnarine 2004).

Although most Jamaican children do not live with their fathers, many fathers do play a part in the lives of their children whether they live with them or not. However, few fathers see nurturing or caregiving as part of their role as fathers. Those who provide support focus on providing the physi-cal necessities such as food, clothing and money for school. Most do not have a clear grasp of their social and intellectual responsibilities toward children (Roopnarine 2004, 75). Most of the students in this study, like the others in their age cohort, live in female headed households. So this fact makes the students in this sample a typical one as far as their household headship is concerned. In comparison to two-parent households, single parents (usually the mother or grandmother), on average, have more limited resources of time, energy and money and are usually less available to the adolescent to provide the guidance and instruction that is necessary at this stage. More importantly, limited financial resources mean that these mothers may have to work more than one job in addition to doing the household chores at home. In such cases, the mother is unable to spend the necessary time listening to or counselling her adolescent child. The stress of overwork and fatigue may cause conflicts in the relationship or may convince the adolescent that the mother has no time for or interest in his or her problems. At the same time, many single parents construct supportive networks but these "aunts" and "uncles" cannot always replace a mother's nurturing.

The parents are often young themselves and were, perhaps, deprived of their own adolescence. They are therefore unable to understand or to empathize with the uncertainties and the difficulties that their youngsters are facing. Psychologically, they are not able to respond patiently to the challenges that adolescents pose. Many parents lacking an understanding of child and adolescent development often respond to their adolescents' behaviour as if it were that of an adult (Brown 2001). They are unable to interpret it or to place it in a context of adolescent development. Additionally, having to face the many economic and social challenges of their own lives, parents' own personal concerns and stresses take precedence. Many of them have also had negative experiences with the school system or are not socially located to dialogue with school personnel or to negotiate for the benefit of their children. For all these reasons, many of these parents are unable to provide supportive and involved parenting, although they all have great ambitions for their children and are often optimistic about the benefits that education will bring.

Parents or parental figures are critical to the social and emotional development of the young adolescent. It is within the family unit and within family relationships that the adolescent learns to manage his or her emotions in positive or negative ways, learns values and the ability to make judgements in the context of particular situations. They learn the cognitive processes that are critical to socialization. What they learn within the family will be critical to the formation of later relationships. The extended family in Jamaica and other parts of the African diaspora, with its network of relatives such as grandparents and aunts, has traditionally provided support to growing adolescents and has been an important avenue for this socialization. This situation of the extended family is now changing, especially for urban youth, because of migration and the young age of grandparents who may still be in the workforce.

Today, socialization takes place in other settings and through new mechanisms. Increasingly, popular culture exerts a strong influence on the imagination of young people with what West (1999) refers to as the "collapsing of structures of meaning, and the collapsing of structures of feeling". The market-driven mass media has now assumed greater salience in instilling values in the young who spend an increasing amount of time watching television (produced in the United States) and listening to music (a sizeable proportion of which also originates in the United States). While some rap and reggae music may attempt to instill certain positive values in young people, other forms, such as dancehall music, may appeal to less salutary values. These artistes now socialize the young in ways once accomplished in Sunday school.

The School in the Life of the Adolescent

The school is the only formal context that the society provides for the socialization of the adolescent and is, next to the family, the most important setting that has an influence on young people. In the case of many of the young adolescents in this study, the school assumes increased salience for students who do not have the close connections and the support of family. Some students in 9X wanted to downplay connections with their own communities which gave the school and the relationships formed there more prominence in their lives. Given the adolescent's stage of development and the sensitive and significant place that this period of adolescence has in the life cycle, the school has a significant impact on the cognitive, social and emotional development of all its students. It aids in the achievement of critical developmental tasks such as forming an appropriate gender role, gaining some degree of emotional maturity and independence, and developing cognitive/academic skills. The school helps to develop character and intellect and also provides the setting for students to develop a sense of efficacy and identity. The school does all this by providing opportunities for students to interact with others; to assume responsibilities that develop capabilities; to engage in actions that have an impact on the environment; and to engage in academic endeavours. All these allow the student to act and to receive feedback. They are therefore able to engage in self-evaluations that contribute to self-development. These activities can also be the occasions when students are treated differently from other students and this can also influence a student's sense of self.

In the Jamaican context, students are treated differently on the basis of gender, class, race, colour and academic ability. At Hillview High School, where students are homogeneous with respect to colour and race, treatment differed mainly by academic ability, gender and class. Academic competence and the student's academic self-concept are critical to his or her functioning in the future. So is the development of emotional maturity and self-acceptance. "The psychosocial implications of academic competence are not only a pivotal resource for positive identity development during adolescence but also for navigating the difficult transition to gainful employment in adulthood" (Swanson, Spencer and Petersen 1998, 31). At the same time, all students have basic psychological needs for belonging, for autonomy and competence (Phillips 1973; Schaps, Battistich and Solomon 1997). The school, comprising teachers, peers and friends, provides opportunities for students to have these needs met.

Adolescents spend five to seven years in high school and are profoundly influenced by this experience. While the school's fundamental objective is to develop its students' literacy and numeracy skills and to provide them with the credentials that are needed for entry into the world of work, as an institution of the society the school has additional obligations. High school, for example, has as one of its functions the provisions of the optimal development of the adolescent student. Yet we know that schools do not always live up to these ideals or expectations. As Goodlad, Mantle-Bromley and Goodlad (2004) state, the concept of education, schooling and teaching are not necessarily good. One has to examine each empirically to make a determination of its goodness.

Challenges Facing Adolescents

Adolescents in Jamaica face various challenges that derive from the contexts in which they live. In situations where there are unfavourable macroeconomic conditions, young people living in poverty are directly affected by adverse economic and social factors. Over the past two decades, many Caribbean countries including Jamaica have "experienced economic decline and stagnation resulting from a loss of preferential treatment in agricultural markets, and losses due to lack of market diversification, stagnation in the manufacturing sector in the face of increased competition, and increasing vulnerability of the tourism sector" (World Bank 2003, 1). These changes at the macro-environmental level have had direct effects not only on government expenditures on education, health and social welfare, but on the household and its disposable income. These conditions usually have a greater impact on the poor than on those in other income groups because they have little to begin with and because they have little to cushion the crisis. They are also disproportionately affected by cuts in government spending on social services (Anderson and Witter 1994, quoted in Barrow 2001, 191). The result is a "pattern of overloaded families, no longer able to protect their weakest and most vulnerable members from economic and social crisis" (Barrow 2001, 193). These deteriorating economic conditions also affect the availability of job opportunities for young people and their perception of education as a means of providing the personal benefits that it once had. These times are thus a period of crisis for youth but especially for youth in poverty.

As adolescents become more cognitively aware, they begin to understand some aspects of the society and their relationship with it. In the case of Jamaica, they become aware of the social stratification and the social differences that mark them off from other social groups. They become keenly aware of the differences in the way they are treated. Many of the young people in this study would have seen their parents and other adult relatives referred to by their first names by children of the middle and upper classes, or may have observed the less deferential treatment of community members within their social class by those of the wealthier classes. Such treatment may negatively affect their sense of self and may fuel rage and resentment. These relations between the classes continue to exist because those in more privileged positions do not regard such issues as problematic and because there have been few avenues for the masses to change their social status. In a recent CARICOM survey of Caribbean youth, more than 40 per cent of adolescents reported having feelings of rage (World Bank 2003, 23). These feelings may stem in part from these social distinctions and the discrimination that they experience. Many working-class youth are discriminated against in their search for employment on the basis of place of residence. Feelings of rage can also stem from their pessimistic view of the future and the treatment that they receive from institutions such as the school. The rage may also stem from being poor in a society where there is conspicuous consumption and an affluent lifestyle among a minority of the population. Males consistently reported rage more often than females in every adolescent age group.

Class

Class is a consideration in this study for two reasons. First, class or socio-economic status has been linked to academic achievement in the education literature and in educational research both locally (Hamilton 1991; Evans 1997) and internationally (Newman 1998). Second, the students who formed part of this study at Hillview High School are largely from working-class or low socio-economic groups. Class therefore is an important variable in this study. Class can be defined as the differentiation of people on the basis of income, occupation and place or type of residence. Such differences are also associated with differences in status and other lifestyle variables related to money and taste.

There is some disagreement as to whether class refers to anything other than a socio-economic grouping. Bryan, in referring to the Jamaican context, states that the use of the term "class" corresponds more with the need to find a convenient term to define a large group of people than with the accurate description of a group that shares common interests, aspirations or consciousness (2000b, 216). Austin, on the other hand, believes that class is inextricably bound up with culture which is a "situational response to an environment and a learnt stylization of behaviour" (1984, xix). Discussions about class often focus on the objective criteria for determining class or the class system or structure and the quantitative aspects of social mobility. The more subjective aspects of class and the existential reality of being in a certain class are not often discussed and are not often taken into account in examining their effects in education (hooks 2000). These more subjective aspects of class are important in any examination of differences in educational achievement or in any attempt to disclose the role of the school in the development of students.

In Jamaica, class has always functioned as a significant aspect of social life and of education, by virtue of the fact that Jamaica is a post-colonial, post-slavery society. This society was founded on inequality with the white race exercising dominance and power over blacks, and denying them basic human and property rights. In post-colonial societies such as Jamaica it is, therefore, difficult to separate class and colour since inequality was based on ethnicity and on whether or not one worked with one's hands (Bryan 2000a, 20). In many respects, Jamaicans live in a world created by the plantation. An important part of this world was and is the social distance between classes – not very different from the social distance that existed between whites and blacks during an earlier period. These differences, however, are always taken for granted and rarely mentioned in public discourse though they inform and affect social relations. The more well-known markers of class are income, occupation, place of residence, manners, behaviour, language, speech, education, dress, the car one drives or whether one takes the bus, to name a few. But the determination of class is never a straightforward matter. Each of the criteria just cited can be modified to a great extent by race, skin colour or ethnicity (Bryan 2000b). Jamaica's class society is based not only on these differences but on structured inequalities of power (Austin 1984). Together with colour groupings, it presents "the major issues of status that constitute a Jamaican sense of hierarchy" (Austin-Broos 2001, 256). The inequalities and the hierarchy are always present and taken for granted in everyday social relations and are rarely mentioned in public discourse. Nevertheless they are always beneath the surface of everyday interactions and discourse, sometimes erupting in cases of conflict or violation of the rules of behaviour.

Class takes on unique aspects in Jamaican society, and Jamaicans have construed the experience of class in particular ways. Based on her ethnographic research in Jamaica over a twenty-year period, Austin-Broos argues that one basis for the social hierarchy that structures social relations is the notion of an inherited difference that subsumes culture, class and race. This notion of "heritable identity", which places an individual in Jamaica's social hierarchy, "brings colour and class together in a variety of different engagements" (2001, 260). The discourse of heritable identity goes beyond class and race and includes education: that which one already has and the possibility or capacity of gaining more. This notion of heritable identity is not as rigid as caste since one can overcome it by means of education. But overcoming this identity is not easy and may take time, maybe generations. As one of Austin-Broos's informants stated, "It took me five generations to be 'educated'. Yu caan tek a chil' from below Torrington Bridge, put 'im in a school and mek 'im 'educated'. Caan be done" (Austin-Broos 2001, 259). For Jamaicans, of course, it takes a much shorter period of time.

At the same time, the discourse on education incorporates the notion of individual achievement, a notion that is tempered with the understanding that opportunities for achievement are few and the constraints are many. In her earlier work, Austin (1984) showed that the ideology of the middle and working classes with respect to education are different. While the middle class believes in education and social mobility, they recognize the constraints and the difficulties that one's cultural inheritance provides. The working class, on the other hand, sees wealth as the determining factor that prevents them from gaining access to education and other benefits of being in the middle class. And so, Jamaican ideas about education and achievement incorporate notions of heritable identity – which places a question mark around the educability of working-class children – while lauding the possibilities of individual achievement. This notion of educability that is linked to social class is a critical one in any examination of student academic achievement. The differences between middle-class and working-class notions of educability and the conditions necessary for gaining an education or becoming educated have implications for student achievement and teachers' views of students' possibilities and potential.

When we examine the ways in which class can affect educational outcomes, we have to examine structural aspects of society and education as well as the complexity of class in everyday life. Regarding structure, the dual system of education has created an unequal education system, with the result that quality education has been accessible mainly to those who attend the traditional high school. According to Austin, the fact that so few of the Jamaican working class have access to quality education means that "the dual system of education, in part inherited from Britain, has made education in the past and still to a great extent in the present, serve the logic of Jamaica's class relations" (1984, xiii). Thus, the dual system has become as prominent as property in organizing Jamaica's class structure. Gordon, in his examination of intergenerational mobility and the educational experiences of young people between 1936 and 1975, found that class origins had a great deal to do with who gets a chance to go to high school in Jamaica. Additionally, he found that the chances of gaining access to high school were also influenced by race, and that the effects of race exist independently of class (1991, 192–93). The advantages of class and race with respect to access to education have been decreasing since 1975, especially in recent years with the expansion of the number of high schools. But the question of access to quality education is still a contentious issue.

Class in everyday life is revealed in complex ways. It is the world of bosses and workers, the rich and the poor, dependency and help seeking, and the existential meanings that these positions and statuses have for individuals. Class shapes the nature of childhood experiences and creates expectations for self and family, ideas about self in relation to others and members of other classes. When students go to school, this class socialization continues. They continue to receive many messages about class, race and colour. Although students' personalities play an important role, class (with its markers of behaviour, dress, manners and speech) also determines the way they respond to and are responded to by teachers and other students, the friendship groups formed, the membership in cliques, and the extent of participation in social activities. In many ways, class inserts itself into the everyday life of the school and is enacted at school in many ways. There are the "haves", who wear the latest clothes and accessories and are driven to school, and the "have nots", who take mini-buses, are treated with disrespect and intolerance, and do not have money for lunch and books.

The relations between teachers and students can, in some circumstances, be affected by class. The teacher's position is one of authority and is based on that individual's knowledge of subject matter, age or formal position in the school. Teachers may be of a different social class than their students by virtue of their achieved status as members of the teaching profession. Yet, as we have seen, there are different markers of class: the achieved markers of education and membership in a profession represent only some of these. Class and class relations are legitimized through ascribable characteristics such as family, socialization, manners and behaviour as well as by achieved status such as education, occupation and wealth. Because some teachers may not be able to acquire some of the ascribable characteristics that are so critical in Jamaican class society (dress, manners, socialization, place of residence and even speech), the social position of some teachers may in fact be quite tenuous or ambiguous. The extent to which this may affect the student-teacher relationship depends on the teacher, the students and the specific circumstances that bring these issues to prominence. As we saw earlier, students' class and social background influence their experience of school not only in Jamaica (Keith 1976; Sistren 1986; Evans 2001) but in other countries such as the United States, Canada and the United Kingdom (Darling-Hammond 1995; Dei et al. 1997). Their schooling experience is strongly influenced by differential teacher expectations; teacher-student interactions; classroom organization such as streaming; the opportunities or lack thereof for students to participate in leadership positions; gender, race and class. Autobiographies reveal that many young people experienced difficulties, and sometimes shame, at school as a result of their class (Thompson 2000; Clarke 1980). hooks (2000), a feminist and cultural studies critic, in reflecting on her years of growing up working class and attending schools in American colleges and universities attended by the rich, recalled that school was also the place where there was class privilege and class shame; where adolescent boys and girls either concealed poverty or flaunted wealth and possessions. For many young people and their parents, "the sense of shame around class was deep and intense" even though it was never talked about. It is possible that the middle classes know less about the feelings and aspirations of the poor than the poor know of the middle classes, since their lifestyle is obvious to all around them and, in many cases, is desired. The poor, who often work in the homes of the privileged, observe these differences and note the extent to which others enjoy an arguably better and easier life.

But what are the specific ways in which class influences a student's academic achievement? The homogeneity of a given student body determines whether students' schooling experiences are differentiated by class. In the case of Hillview High School, since most students are from a poor working-class background, such differentiation may not be as evident and may not have as great an effect on students and their academic achievement. Data from this study may throw light on the spheres in which the conflicts and the tensions of the wider society are played out in schools which are "contested public spheres, political sites for the reproduction of power and social inequality" (Giroux 1996). These are the salient issues that framed the study and which influenced the research design.

Notes

1. The Reform of Secondary Education (ROSE) was a major innovation implemented in 1993. ROSE aims to increase access to secondary education, improve the quality of education and, consequently, to increase equality of educational opportunity. Quality will be achieved by means of a revised common curriculum for all types of secondary high schools and new teaching methods that are more participatory.

2. See King (1998, 1999) for a review of the legacy of the nineteenth century and the origins of educational inequality in access and quality as well as differences in the curriculum offered.

3. In 2002, enrolment in grade 6 in all public primary schools stood at 48,284. Yet, in that year, there were only 34,672 enrolled in grade 7 of the high schools. So, approximately one-third of graduates of the primary schools do not get placed in the high schools, because there are not enough places at grade 7 in these high schools. Some of these grade 6 students remain in the all-age schools which terminate at grade 9. Only one-fourth of all primary-school graduates get placed in the traditional high schools.

4. Although schools within each of these categories vary in quality and academic achievement of their students, the results of the regional CXC examinations in 2002 showed that 49 per cent of students in traditional high schools passed the Mathematics examination compared with 16 per cent of those in the upgraded high schools. In the case of English Language, the pass rates were 54 per cent for the traditional high schools compared with 37 per cent for the upgraded high schools.

5. Admission to high schools, since 1999, has been based on parental choice of schools and an examination called the Grade Six Achievement Test (GSAT). This examination is based on the curriculum of the primary school in contrast to the previous test, the Common Entrance Examination, which was an intelligence test. On the application for this examination, parents are allowed to indicate a choice of three high schools. Students are then assigned to their first, second or third choice depending on the availability and the grade obtained on the GSAT. Those who obtain a high mark on the GSAT are given first choice and so have first choice of the high status schools. Those students who obtain a low mark on the GSAT are often assigned to schools that they did not choose.

Chapter 3   School, Teachers and Curriculum

Hillview High School is located in a middle-class area of Kingston with views of the hills of Kingston visible from every corner of the campus. Established in 1979 as a new secondary school, Hillview was reclassified as a high school nine years later. As indicated earlier, the establishment of new secondary schools was part of the drive to expand secondary education in the post-independence era. With the reclassification of these schools to high school status, access to high school education was widened. There were now more high schools and more students eligible for admission and there was also a simultaneous change in method of admission to these high schools. Nevertheless, these policy changes did not immediately result in a change in the quality of education in these schools and the public's perceptions of the schools' quality and value. The public has continued to regard the upgraded high schools as lacking in quality, and so they are not the favoured choice of parents. Because of the nature of the admission process to secondary schools, with placement being influenced by parental choice as well as performance on the GSAT, students at Hillview High School continue to be mainly from the low socio-economic group. For the same reason, students come from all geographical sections of Kingston and even from areas far afield, such as Bull Bay in the neighbouring parish of St Thomas.

When the school was established in 1979, there was some resistance from the well-established middle-class community. Many of the residents objected to having a school built in their immediate environs. Because the children of the middle-class community who live adjacent to the school do not attend this school, there has not been a close and ongoing working relationship between the school and the community. Sporadic interest has been paid from time to time, as was seen when a group of residents offered a set of drums for garbage disposal to the school when they saw that this was necessary. But, overall, there is little interaction between Hillview and the surrounding community, despite the fact that there are opportunities where the immediate community could contribute in important ways to the functioning and development of the school.

The Parent-Teacher Association is an important part of a school community. When this association is vibrant and interested in the affairs of the school, it can make a significant contribution to the goals of that school by providing financial support when needed and by making other contributions in kind. It can also be supportive of the curriculum, helping students with homework or providing the necessary materials and resources for learning. In the case of Hillview High School, the effective functioning of the Parent-Teacher Association is stymied for three main reasons. First, most parents may find it difficult to make it to the meetings as they live a long way from the school. Additionally, some hold skilled and semi-skilled jobs which require them to work at odd hours of the day, thereby making it difficult for them to participate in the affairs of the school on an ongoing basis. Second, parents' social distance (as working-class individuals) from teachers and administrators (who would be termed middle class) also affects their involvement in school affairs and in the school-related activities of their children. A third reason relates to some parents' lack of financial resources. Most parents of Hillview's student population are low-income earners with little job security. In times of retrenchment in the economy, which has occurred in Jamaica's recent past, these persons can easily join the ranks of the unemployed. And, indeed, there are parents who are unemployed who have children attending Hillview High School. Although the poverty line set by governmental agencies in 2002 was J\$47,128.70 (or roughly US\$80.00 per person per annum), and the estimate of Jamaicans living in poverty was 16.9 per cent (STATIN 2002b), the incidence of poverty is much higher.

The School

The campus of Hillview High School is fairly large, but one-half of it is allocated to a football field that is equal in size to the area on which the classrooms are located. Despite its small size, the main campus is designed so that there are walking areas and spaces separating the blocks of classrooms. On entering the campus from the parking lot, there is a circular area bordered by a block of classrooms and specialist sections such as the library, the computer room and the administrative blocks. To the left of the entrance to the campus is the main administrative block. Within the central area, there is an auditorium and some green spaces and walkways where students make their way from one side of the circle to the other. Around this inner circle of rooms and centres is another circle where most of the classrooms are located. The school has built additional classrooms between these two circles of classrooms to accommodate the increasing student population. Rooms have been added on to other rooms in areas that were originally open spaces. These additions give an appearance of congestion, especially during recess and lunch.

When asked what they liked about their school, the students of Hillview High focused on the staff and students and rarely mentioned the school site itself. When prompted, they said they would like the grounds and bathrooms to be better kept. Also, the kind of things they want at school indicates what is now missing: a canteen or lunch room, a rest room, a bathroom with a shower (which would come in handy after physical education classes), a garden, some greenery, perhaps a swimming pool (this said with a laugh). Some students are pleased with the community and the location of the school. "It's peaceful. I can just sit down, pick up a book and do a little work." Some like travelling the distance from their homes to get to school as it gives them a chance to be away from their communities.

The Academic Staff

Currently, there is a great deal of focus on the teacher as the agent of reform in many countries, including Jamaica. It is increasingly recognized that the improvement of teaching, and of education in general, rests with the teacher and his or her subject matter, pedagogical skills, and commitment to teaching and to students (Darling-Hammond 1999, 2001). In contemporary Jamaica the spotlight has been turned on teachers, especially high school teachers, and there is currently much discussion about the quality of teachers and the ways in which teaching can be improved.

There are fifty-five teachers on the staff of the school; this number includes a principal, a vice-principal, two guidance counsellors and a dean of discipline. Most of the teachers have a diploma in teaching, which is the type of certificate awarded at the end of the three-year programme at a teachers' college. Some teachers have a bachelor's degree and a few have a master's degree or are enrolled in a master's programme. Only two teachers were untrained: one in the area of science. The experience of the staff was also varied, with most having less than ten years experience. The eleven teachers included in this study (in their capacity as teachers of grade 9X) had experience ranging from five years to twenty-two years.

Like most high schools, Hillview is organized on a departmental basis. There are eight departments, each with a head who has general responsibility for organizing the academic work of the department and for supervising teaching. The main work of the school is therefore carried out within the departments. There are also grade-level supervisors who coordinate the work at each grade level; make decisions regarding the students in that grade; maintain records; address disciplinary problems; and organize and plan programmes with teachers for the benefit of the students. Each class is assigned a form teacher who is organizationally the closest faculty member to the students. That form teacher normally meets with students each day during form time (a scheduled session) when the class may choose to do whatever is of benefit to the group. For example, the students may choose to plan a class trip or discuss a current problem or issue of concern to most or all students. Form teachers may be promoted to the level of senior teacher which would require them to perform extra duties.

Most of the teachers in the study had always wanted to teach, liked teaching and could not see themselves doing anything else. In some cases, there was a family member who was also a teacher. These are the reasons they gave for becoming a teacher:[1]

> I guess growing up, I always wanted to be a teacher. I was made to be one. It runs in the family. My father was a teacher and one of my aunts too.
>
> I think for me, [being] a teacher is innate. I always wanted to be a teacher.
>
> I can't see myself doing anything else. I keep saying what would I do now? And I love the students.

Like many who enter teaching, some teachers simply fell into teaching and then grew to like it.

> It's something you just fall into. The thing is, I like teaching.

The Formal Curriculum

The formal academic curriculum began at 8:10 a.m. and ended at 2:35 p.m. During those six hours and twenty-five minutes, students attended classes which were structured into nine periods of thirty-five minutes each. There were some double periods for some subjects such as English language, English literature and social studies and triple periods for resource and technology. Lunch lasted for slightly more than an hour. Attendance at classes took up much of the students' academic time at school. Short transitions occurred between timetabled periods allowing students to prepare for the next class.

The written curriculum which, in Jamaica, is common to all secondary schools, represents only what the school intends for students to learn and what teachers are supposed to teach. According to Doyle (1992, 492), "it stands outside classrooms as a definition of the purposes and contents of schooling". This written curriculum is different from the enacted or experienced curriculum where teachers and students come together to engage in teaching and learning. At this level, the curriculum cannot be conceptualized without considering the students, the materials and resources used in teaching and the pedagogical methods used to get students to learn. This experienced curriculum can only be understood in reference to the physical classroom context and the social context in which it is embedded.

One of the aims of Hillview High School, as described in the school's brochure, is to "expose students to a wide range of choices in both the practical as well as the academic areas to enable them to acquire relevant skills". And so there is a balance of academic and practical subjects offered to students. In the school's information brochure, twelve academic subjects and fifteen practical subjects are listed as being offered by the school. The curriculum of the academic subjects is similar to that offered in all Jamaican high schools, for the same curriculum is now prescribed for all high schools in Jamaica. For the first three years, all high schools follow the ROSE (Reform of Secondary Education) curriculum. This programme was introduced in 1993 and later extended to all secondary schools in 1999.

The academic subjects offered at the grade 9 level are English language, English literature, mathematics, social studies, religious education and Spanish. The practical subjects offered at this grade level are principles of accounts, music, physical education, resource and technology, and information technology. Family life education and library were timetabled once per week. These last two subjects are additional offerings made available because the school considers them necessary. At grade 10, students begin the CXC programme which extends for two years and culminates in the CXC examination. They may also begin the Secondary School Certificate programme, which is an alternative to the CXC for those who are not considered academically capable of mastering the CXC curriculum.

The curriculum guide describes the goals and outlines the content or subject matter that students are expected to learn, and makes suggestions about teaching methods. These methods reflect a student-centred and progressive approach to teaching. Materials and resources provide an elaboration of subject matter and serve as a reference for students seeking to understand concepts. It is in part through such materials that the curriculum is made manifest to students. The materials that teachers can use in the classroom include textbooks, posters or other visual materials, tests, worksheets, videotapes, film, recordings, the internet and computer programmes. Materials such as these represent the content or subject matter that students encounter.

These materials however are simply a source of knowledge about curriculum content. For all students to learn that content in a meaningful way, it has to be represented, and not simply presented, to students in ways that are meaningful to them. Representing knowledge in meaningful ways requires pedagogical skills, whether they are general or specific to a particular topic. In representing content with student understanding in mind, the teacher has to take into account the learners' perspective or ways of thinking as they relate to a particular topic or unit. It requires an awareness of students' background knowledge, experiences and preconceptions (which sometimes act as misconceptions). Researchers who subscribe to a constructivist approach to learning emphasize the mental processes that the learner engages in while constructing or creating meaning: processes such as comparing, applying, deducing and concluding. To enable this construction of knowledge, the teacher has to be aware of or be prepared to elicit the understandings, skills or conceptions that students already have.

The curriculum that students encounter is represented in tasks to be accomplished. These tasks are meaningful because they may engage students' cognitive abilities or they may simply require memorization. Doyle (1983, 161) describes it thus:

> the term task focuses attention on three aspects of students' work: a) the products students are to formulate, such as an original essay or answers to a set of test questions; b) the operations that are to be used to generate the product, such as memorizing a list of works or classifying examples of a concept; and c) the "givens" or resources available to students while they are generating a product such as a model of a finished essay supplied by the teacher or a fellow student. Academic tasks, in other words, are defined by the answers students are required to produce and the routes that can be used to obtain these answers.

Tasks, therefore, form the core unit of a curriculum and teachers have to design tasks in order for students to experience the curriculum. One can distinguish between *task content* which refers to the goals and subject matter, and *task form* which refers to the activities engaged in; their procedural complexity; and the social organization required for its completion. Task form has implications for student motivation to engage in and complete the task (Doyle 1992) since it specifies whether there will be an activity, and whether this activity will be carried out individually or in a group. A teacher can design a task in which the task content is easy or difficult, and in which the task form is organizationally complex or simple; requires group or individual work; or uses a wide or limited range of materials. Tasks reveal the level at which students engage in cognitive processes, and influence learning by directing their attention to particular aspects of the content and of the lesson. Tasks frame both pedagogy and the curriculum because they specify the ways in which academic work and thus cognition is organized and examine how students process information. To capture the curriculum in use, one must describe the tasks enacted with respect to that curriculum. The nature and use of instructional materials and textbooks are central to the nature of the tasks and the representation of the curriculum. Students inevitably have to do some interpretation of a task or the instructions associated with a task in order to complete it, and the ease with which students do this depends on a variety of factors. The enactment of the curriculum, the nature of the tasks provided and students' interpretation of these tasks will be examined in the next chapter.

Extra-Curricular Activities

Extra-curricular activities play an important part in the overall development of the high school student. These activities and the informal peer group are the major extra-classroom contexts that influence the adolescent (Brown and Theobald 1998). The prefix *extra* before curricular suggests, to some, that these activities are different from and perhaps less important than the academic curriculum which they view as the main programme of the school. Some use the term co-curricular activities to signal that they are as important as the curricular programme to the overall development of the student. Whatever the view held of the role and importance of these activities, they form a part of the offerings of all high schools. While their importance is recognized, the participation of staff and students in these activities varies from school to school.

Hillview High School regards these activities as fulfilling a part of the mission of the school: that is, to encourage and facilitate the development of a rounded individual and to provide quality education for all students through a variety of curricular and extra-curricular activities. Students are required to become involved in at least one activity. Most activities are offered after school, which is a common practice in Jamaican high schools. The extra-curricular activities which are listed in the academy's brochure are divided into two categories: Physical Education and Games, and Other Extra-Curricular Activities. Under Physical Education and Games are the following: athletics, basketball, cricket, football, hockey, lawn tennis, netball, table tennis and volleyball. Under the category of Other Extra-Curricular Activities are: choir, dancing, debate, drama, 4-H, ISCF (Inter-Varsity Christian Fellowship), Key Club (a subdivision of Kiwanis International), Spanish Club, Quiz, Tourism Action Club and Octagon Club (a subdivision of Optimist International). The school's brochure also states that "students are encouraged to participate in sports and extra-curricular activities, in order to become well-rounded people".

The administration readily admits that some of these clubs are more active than others. The problem may be due as much to student interest, ability or willingness to attend after-school activities as it is teacher availability to supervise these activities. Form teachers are expected to explain the benefits of such participation to their students and to encourage student participation. They are ideally suited to do this as their relationship with the students of a given class is more intimate and ongoing. In addition, there is a teacher assigned to each club who acts as the faculty representative for that club. There is a gender difference in the participation of students in sports activities, with boys being more actively involved in sports such as basketball, football and athletics and girls participating more actively in netball and hockey. This school boasts a very strong girls' hockey team.

In addition to these extra-curricular activities, older students are also offered developmental opportunities through their activities as prefects and their participation in the Student Council. Prefects who are members of the council are given responsibilities for enforcing school rules and monitoring school activities, such as overseeing the lunch line and handling students' tardiness. Prefects are also assigned to a class and are responsible for ensuring that they adhere to school rules. The council meets on a regular basis to discuss aspects of the functioning of the school and the areas such as discipline that falls in their purview. Teachers are also assigned to the council and are expected to engage students in various activities and experiences that build leadership skills. Both teachers and students in the council are able to plan special activities that provide developmental opportunities for students.

The Classroom

To get to 9X from the school entrance, one may walk along the corridor in front of the administrative block and cross an open space to a second corridor off which the 9X classroom is located. The corridor in front of the administrative block is supposed to be off limits to students. However, because the office of one of the guidance counsellors is on this block, students who come for consultation with him are often seen waiting along this corridor. There are no trees or plants on the path between the two corridors and, during the period of observation, the ground was usually parched, making the entrance to 9X very dusty. On many of my visits, I was met with a swirl of dust as a student swept the classroom and then swept that section of the corridor in front of 9X. A culvert runs along the other side of the corridor, and on the other side of it, directly opposite 9X, is another classroom. This is one of those classrooms that was added on to make space for the growing number of students admitted to Hillview High School over the years and was constructed in an area that was once an open space. Sounds from this room and rooms on either side of 9X could be heard within the 9X classroom. Thus, the surrounding environment of Room 9X was usually filled with activity and sounds of various sorts, sometimes muffled, sometimes loud. Unexpected sounds might suddenly erupt from any of these three classrooms in close proximity to Class 9X. However, the students in 9X rarely seemed disturbed by this as they had apparently become accustomed to the external noise.

The classroom was of average size – roughly fifteen feet by fifteen feet. There were forty-two students on roll and usually only one or two students were absent. The classroom, therefore, appeared crowded. There were seven columns of desks and chairs with five, six or seven students seated in each column. The columns were close to each other, but it was possible to walk along the spaces between columns if one was careful to pay attention to protruding legs, books or bags on the floor, and desks that were usually out of line. The space between the first and second column nearest to the entrance to the left was wider than the others, and this was where teachers entered and walked to the front of the room and to the teachers' desk which was in the right hand corner at the front of the room. Students whose seats were located in these first two columns to the left also used this space to enter and exit. The other students used the limited space at the back of the room to move in and out and around.

During the first term, the walls were decorated with posters obtained from various agencies that promoted a healthy lifestyle. There were five posters, all chosen by Mr Lawrence, the form teacher, whose wish it was to decorate the class and to send positive messages at the same time. On my first visit, when I mentioned the posters to him, he replied, "Mine is the only class with posters on the wall." One poster depicted young people at the beach having a good time with the words below: "Since life so nice"; another exhorted the reader to "keep your dreams alive. Respect yourself. Stay drug free"; while another poster was about domestic violence, depicting a man assaulting a woman. Mr Lawrence said that he regularly talked to the students about physically assaulting each other and about the importance of self-control. He knew that such behaviour was common in the communities from which these students came and he had often seen anger erupt unexpectedly in 9X.

The room contained a fan that was always on and windows on the left and right. To the right of the room there were horizontal louvres extending the height of the room. A small opening near the top provided additional ventilation. Near the teachers' desk, there was also a window with a grill on the outside and with most of the louvres missing. From this window one could look out onto the field and teachers were often observed doing this as the students carried out seatwork. On the left of the classroom, there were similar openings in the wall and windows. Unfortunately, however, the room was always hot. This may have been one of the reasons why some students seemed lethargic and unable to give the lessons their full attention. In my field notes there were many references to the heat and its effect on students, for example, "It is quite hot in the classroom. No wonder students are sleeping", or "The teacher tries to awaken a boy who is sleeping." When asked what they would like to change about the school, one group of students agreed with the sentiments expressed by Jean:

> How the classrooms are made. [It is] really tormenting. Sometimes after lunch I want to go to the door because in the class, it is just too hot for you to stay there. When it is hot, sometimes you are not really listening to what the teacher is saying. Sometimes the students fight to sit near the window because they know a little breeze is coming.

Another feature that could not escape the notice of an outside observer was the constant noise level. This noise, when caused by the misbehaviour of fellow students, was an irritant to many students. There was usually some kind of inappropriate noise made at all times throughout the course of the day – during lessons, while students waited for the teacher, during transitions between activities, and at the start and end of the day. As an observer, I sometimes had difficulty hearing what was being said by teacher and students alike. The noise came from adjoining classrooms as well as from the students in 9X. The noise, usually in the form of talking that became disruptive, would occasionally ebb as the teacher intervened or as the matter causing the disturbance was resolved. Some students responded to sounds for a brief moment and then returned to their work. Others seemed not to notice. As an observer, I made frequent comments on the noise level in the field notes. For example: "There is so much noise, I can hardly hear. I go next door to see if the noise is coming from there, but it isn't." And, "The teacher is shouting instructions which I cannot hear because of the din."

The disruption was caused mainly by a minority of students. Students and teachers admitted that once a disruption occurred, it was sometimes difficult to regain the tenor and flow of the lesson. Class 9X had had a reputation for being restless, noisy and disruptive since their entry to grade 7. This reputation can be said to have negatively influenced the attitude of some of their teachers. As one group of students said during the interview, "Sometimes the teacher comes and says, 'I need better from you', and sometimes they come in and say nothing at all. And most of the time, they tell us that other classes are better than us." However, some teachers continued to be encouraging, exhorting 9X students to demonstrate good behaviour and communicating high expectations despite students' seeming unwillingness to change.

Teachers usually punished the miscreant if he or she was known, and if not, they punished the entire class. This did not go down well with many students as this girl explained: "Well I think it is really disgusting because the good suffer for the bad, because when one does something bad, the others get detention. So everybody gets punished everyday." The students who were not involved in these noisy disruptions responded in a number of ways: Molly trained herself "to concentrate because I have to live with it", Susan would "just sit down and block out. I just fold my hand and think about other things." Others tried to ignore the noise because there was no alternative.

And yet these students admitted that at times the noise was a welcome change from a lesson that failed to capture their interest.

> Jean: Like sometime, if the teacher is not here, they will liven up the class, or if the teacher is there and is not saying anything, they liven it up, but sometimes they speak out of turn.

> Nadine: Sometimes I just start throwing paper around in class. Torment the kids.

> Julien: If the lesson is boring, then we just feel like talking.

There were also students who admitted that the noise did not disturb them since they were accustomed to studying with background noise, such as music, at home.

> O'Neill: Sometimes I'm in the mood for noise. I get accustomed to the noise when I'm studying, when I do my work.

But most students admitted that the noise often created confusion in the classroom and limited their ability to concentrate. As Andrew remarked, "Sometimes there is too much confusion going on."

Note

1. These quotations were taken from interviews with teachers.

Chapter 4   Teaching and Learning:
                The Hope and the Reality

Students' Expectations

What students liked most about Hillview High School was the teachers. High school students have had at least six years of experience being taught by teachers at the primary level. Therefore, they come to high school with perceptions of the role and status of teachers, and the students of 9X were no exception. They had definite expectations about their teachers, which they expressed in different contexts in response to various questions. Students responded in several ways – some seriously, some angrily, some laughingly. However, some clear themes emerged. Students expected teachers to teach for understanding; to teach in an interesting way; to believe in and care for students; to be willing to encourage and motivate students; to be a friend or an approachable person; and to embody certain personal qualities.

Teaching for Understanding

Teaching for understanding was a common theme that was mentioned by many students in the interviews. This was how some of them expressed the idea (all quotations below are taken from interviews with students):

> Teach so that students understand [and can] pick up on what you are saying.
>
> Break it down simply, miss.
>
> Go over what is not understood.
>
> Talk to the children about the work, so that the way you say it, they understand.
>
> Teachers should give help after class if you do not understand.

Here students are talking about the teacher's responsibility to help students to learn no matter what, even if it means giving extra tutoring after class. For them, explaining clearly, breaking down content for understanding, posing questions on what is learned and being willing to give extra time to clear up misunderstandings are basic obligations that teachers should fulfil.

Teaching in an Interesting Way

Teaching in an interesting way was another major theme and was mentioned more frequently than teaching for understanding. Students expected their teachers not only to teach so that they understand but to do fun activities, and not be boring. As one student said, "Interest is a major part of it." This is what they had to say about teaching in an interesting way:

> If you are doing a subject and you're not interested in it, then your mind not there for it. But if it is interesting, that's different.
>
> Do things that we really can enjoy. Some of these teachers, they just come in, teach, just do what they are told to do. They don't make sure that the class participate and although they're learning, they're having fun learning.
>
> It all depends on the vibes of the teacher to make that subject interesting because if it's not interesting, the children feel a way; they don't even want to listen to the teacher. That's why sometimes the children in the class are sleeping. The teacher is teaching and it don't have any vibes, any feeling to make a student want to get up and listen to it.

Belief in and Caring for Students

Belief in and caring for students was a third theme evident in students' conversations. This seemed to be an emotional issue for students, as most who expressed this view spoke with much feeling and at length to get the point across. In some cases, examples were used to show caring and non-caring attitudes of teachers. This is how the students expressed this idea:

> Believe that we can fulfil our dreams and excel. Believing in us is very important.
>
> They want us to become somebody.
>
> Show the students respect and that I [the teacher] care about them.
>
> She can show us that she care that we learning. If she doesn't care, why should we . . .?
>
> To care for us and give us the best education.

Encouraging and Motivating

Encouraging and motivating students was a fourth theme evident in students' responses. Here, students are referring to the teacher's going beyond mere teaching (even for understanding) and getting students to want to learn, by using encouraging words, or by showing belief in the students' abilities. In some respects, the sentiments are almost similar to those expressed in the third theme of believing in or caring for students, or they are a manifestation of a teacher's caring. In other words, teachers who care for students also encourage and motivate them. This is how some students expressed it:

> They should try to motivate us – especially those who are not doing so well.
>
> They should encourage us, make us want to learn.

Being Approachable

Students also needed *someone in whom they could confide*: "someone who can be a friend – like a father or mother", or "someone who can act as our parent". These contradictory sentiments really reflect these students' need to discuss the many issues that they face at home, at school and in their community. It also suggests that, for many of them, their parents were not available physically or emotionally. Those students who expressed this view talked about having someone in whom they could confide. However, as we will see later, this was a wish realized only with their form teacher, who became for all of them a substitute parent, big brother, uncle, guide and friend.

Embodying Special Qualities

Finally, students wanted teachers who had certain personal qualities. A teacher should show respect to students and of course should be someone whom students can respect. They should send out "positive energy to get what she want from you", and they should be able to "run a joke with you from time to time". "They can't just teach, teach, teach."

These were students' expectations for their teachers. These expectations, however, were rarely met, whether with respect to the act of teaching or the teacher-student relationship.

Students' Views on Good Teaching

Implicit in students' expectations of teachers was their view of good teaching or what a good teacher did. They were also asked explicitly about teaching and to make suggestions that would improve teaching at Hillview High School. The following questions were asked: What are your teachers like? How do you feel about them? What do you look for in a teacher? What is an interesting class like? What are some of the things that make a lesson really good or interesting? If you were to teach your classes for a week, what kinds of things would you do or let your students do? Most of their comments had to do with pedagogy – what teachers and students did during a learning activity. But they also spoke of the teachers' personal qualities and the relationships that teachers should have with their students. The comments below elaborate on their expectations of teachers.

Participatory Teaching

Many students wished for learning to be participatory, that is, based on activities that involved students. In describing this kind of teaching they related, often in an animated fashion, experiences they had had with former teachers.

> In eighth grade, we did a lot of experiments. But since we come into ninth grade, we don't have that. In eighth grade, we would do the experiments and understand more. We get the notes and with the experiment, we understand more.

> More activities. And practical activities – not just sitting down and writing; exploring more than that. . . . Let [students] have a little skit to interest them.

> You could take them on a field trip, like if they are doing a particular topic, take them to a place related to that topic.

> Have quiz. Have competition. Let them have a little skit to interest them.

At times, this activity could be a form of experiential learning. For instance, one student describing a class that she had found meaningful and interesting, said, "We'd pretend we're all lawyers and trying to figure out a case. Learning how to be a lawyer, write a case, [be] a judge making decisions."

In addition to activities in which they could participate, students felt that learning activities should also be interesting and fun, as was outlined earlier. To make a lesson interesting, they thought music could add to the quality of the learning experience in addition to making it fun.

> Use music when teaching – children learn more, because most people like it.

> I would do it through music. I would have a little song prepared. Anything.

> I notice children are attracted to music.

> Mr ——— was one of the best ——— teachers we ever had. He made us understand it very good. He used songs and used interesting activities.

> He knows that if we don't understand something, most of us won't pay it any mind. So he tries to lively up the class. . . . He would use some reggae tunes and then add to the Spanish.

Good teaching required the teacher to give clear explanations of ideas, so that students could understand. This meant the use of vocabulary that is at the students' level, the breaking down of subject matter into manageable portions so that students could take it in, or using alternative approaches when one does not seem to work.

> They should try to explain things easier.
>
> They should teach in two different ways because some people would understand it one way and some people would understand it another way.
>
> Make sure they understand everything you say to them – like some words, put it inna fi dem meaning, mek dem more fully understand.
>
> Explain it to them and find something fun that they would like in that lesson and then go on to the hard part and try to explain to them.

And if the students still did not understand, they expected the teacher to try alternative approaches to ensure that students grasp the concept. A student spoke of a teacher who did this:

> She teaches for us to understand. If there is a particular part that we don't understand, she lets us discuss it and she writes questions on the board and we answer them and then, after, she will discuss it again so that we understand. So that even if you don't study for a test, you have it in your mind.

Students also felt that teachers should review and check for students' understanding: "They should always ask when they finish a subject if anyone doesn't understand." A student related an example of a teacher who did this, "If you get something wrong he go over it. Even the next day him come back to it first."

Some students wanted teachers to use students' experiences and ideas when teaching. In the next quote, Molly refers to interactive teaching in which there is an exchange between teacher and student and the teacher takes students' definitions and viewpoints into account in furthering the discussion: "I guess they should try to listen to us more, to seek our opinions on things rather than just telling us and expect us to just keep it – not say anything."

In addition to what the teacher does when teaching, students spoke about their personal qualities as well as the relationship they established with students.

Strict when it comes on to book work. Fun teacher. Have a lot of confidence in us. Believe that we can fulfil our dreams and excel.

Show my students respect and that I care about them. And that I want to see them come to something in life

Deal with them more friendly. This teacher she take everything seriously. She just boring.

The teacher in grade 8, she was kinda strict. But she was all right. She will let us learn and show us respect and laugh with us. She was strict differently.

So students had definite ideas about how a good teacher should teach. These images were based on their experiences with former teachers, and were based on activities that they liked as students. They may also have been based on what they had found to be helpful in their own learning.

Much of what students identified as desirable learning activities has been shown to be related to student learning and student achievement in the educational literature (Darling-Hammond 2000; Perkins 2004). Students learn more when they are actively engaged in the learning activity, when they are allowed to express their ideas, when the teacher includes their experiences in the learning process, when the teacher checks for understanding, when the teacher holds high expectations for students, and establishes a warm and non-threatening learning environment. These have been the findings of research informed by different theoretical perspectives on the nature of learning, the construction of meaning, the quality of the learning environment and the effects of teachers' expectations on students' motivation. From the students' perspective, however, they were recalling moments when they had learned in a meaningful way and had enjoyed the learning process.

In these discussions about good teaching, students could not avoid making reference to the aspects of teaching of which they disapproved. In many ways they were saying that such behaviours did not exemplify good teaching.

Not have us just sitting down and writing.

They come in the class, write it on the blackboard, then they explain it and some of them start shout at the students.

Curriculum Tasks and Students'
Cognitive Processes in the Classroom

In an earlier chapter, the curriculum was described and the importance of curriculum tasks discussed. The tasks translate what is contained in the curriculum guide into activities. They specify the subject matter and the ways in which students will interact with that subject matter. Instructional materials, including the textbooks, are critical in designing tasks as these are the materials with which students interact while learning.

The textbook was used by students in six (25 per cent) of the twenty-four lessons observed. In fourteen of the other eighteen lessons, or roughly 58 per cent of the lessons observed, students did not have the use of a textbook. Furthermore, in most lessons observed, there was an absence of instructional materials. The result was that the content of the lesson or the instructions for completing an assignment were read or written on the chalkboard for students to copy down and work out in their notebooks. On several occasions when I arrived to observe a class, the chalkboard was filled with information which could readily be found in a textbook. This information was outlined as it was in the textbook, but often presented in a simplified form. As this was usually the only source of content for the majority of these students, this limited students' access to knowledge. There was thus a heavy reliance on the word taken directly from the text and written on the chalkboard. In the remaining four lessons, instructional materials (for example, a poem) were circulated, drawings were made on the chalkboard, and test results were distributed and discussed.

So how, specifically, did teachers manage to teach without instructional aids or textbooks? As mentioned earlier, there was a heavy reliance on writing the information on the chalkboard or the teacher reading it from the textbook or presenting it orally to students. The following describes what students were asked to do, and what materials were available in the twenty-four lessons observed.

Do seatwork, filling in the blanks in incomplete sentences written on chalkboard	3
Check answers to test items written on chalkboard	2
No textbook; teacher draws illustration on chalkboard and explains. Students write the information in their notebooks	2

Information written on chalkboard; students write what is written in their notebook	5
No textbook or instructional materials. Students listen and write what is said in their notebooks	3
Read from textbooks and answer questions (in one lesson most answers could be delivered verbatim from the textbook)	5
Students provided with instructional materials (though in one lesson, they were insufficient for number of students) and work cooperatively in groups	2
Students assigned materials and work on an assignment that requires problem solving	2

In this outline of the twenty-four lessons observed, we see the nature of the tasks assigned, the products or learning outcomes envisaged, the cognitive processes engaged in, and the resources and materials at students' disposal. In the majority of cases, students either listened and recorded notes or engaged in lower levels of thinking such as recall of information or memorization. In other lessons, students were engaged in thinking processes that required some comprehension and analysis during the recitation format. And there were four lessons where students engaged in higher-order levels of thinking.

An example of the first category of lessons (where students either listened and recorded notes, or engaged in lower levels of thinking such as recall of information or memorization) follows. This is demonstrated in a lesson in which the teacher relied on a drawing on the chalkboard and his explanation of the content as the main source of knowledge about the subject matter. In this lesson, students admitted at the end that they did not understand, as seen in the extract below:

1:45 p.m.	Teacher begins to draw a diagram on the chalkboard.
1:50 p.m.	Teacher turns around and says, "9X, be quiet." As he draws, the talking continues.
2:00 p.m	Teacher is still drawing and writing. He has his back turned to the class.
	A boy comes over to me to quietly make a comment on his teaching.
	Teacher: Be quiet.

2:03 p.m.	Teacher finishes, turns around and looks at the students. (He has spent seventeen minutes drawing.)
	Teacher asks: "Have you taken down the diagram?" Remember we talked about X. He continues to explain X, using examples.
	Teacher explains and then asks, "It makes sense?"
	Students: "No!"
2:10 p.m.	"All right, let's walk through it. Class! Let's walk through."
	He reads what he has written on the chalkboard. He "walks through" as he said he would, reading and pointing to the diagram.
	Teacher, still holding the book in his hand, asks, "Any questions?"
	Students: "No."
	Teacher: "Remember what we said about Y——?"
	Students: "Yes, sir." "No, sir."

(Field notes, 22 April 2004)

The operations or thinking processes required of the students had to do with reading and repeating rather than thinking and reasoning. The emphasis on these lower levels of thinking can be explained in part by the absence of the instructional materials or textbooks, which in turn limited the nature of the learning tasks that students could engage in. There are problems of learning in this manner. Students do not engage in any mental process that allows them to comprehend, reason, interact with and interrogate the material, or relate to their own experiences or present understanding, which would allow them to learn in a meaningful way. The problem of learning in this way is that students very often do not really understand the basic concepts taught, and later have difficulty in representing the knowledge.

In the lesson described above, the task form emphasized individual work, with activities limited to listening, comprehending and writing. Since students were not required to work on a product, there was no need to communicate these outcomes to the teacher or for students to communicate among themselves about how to carry out the task or discuss the outcome of the task, and so there was no need for feed-back. The task form appeared very simple. The problem is that it did not engage students' interest and motivate them. Judging this lesson using Doyle's (1983) set of criteria for curriculum tasks, it can be said to have fallen short: there was no clear goal for students' learning outcomes other than to memorize the content, no instructional material or textbook other than the diagram the teacher drew on the chalkboard, there were limited operational processes involving listening to and recalling information.

In the second category of lessons observed, students were asked questions which were most usually answered verbatim from the textbook. This is illustrated in the following extract.

> 10:15 a.m.   The teacher begins the lesson. She writes on the chalkboard "Categories of Workers". She refers to what students learned the last time and directs them to page 49 of their textbook. She asks them to read the heading.
>
> They read: "Professional, Official and Technical Workers". She corrects some pronunciation.
>
> Teacher: "Can you give me an example of these types of workers?"
>
> All hands are up. Students are called upon. They seem quite eager. They call out "librarian", "director" and so on.
>
> I then take a peek at the page and realize these examples of workers are written in the book.
>
> (Field notes, 3 October 2003)

In lessons such as this one, students did not have to work on a product or learning outcome. They engaged in the discussion and recorded notes in their notebooks.

In the third category of lessons, students engaged in higher-order levels of thinking as the curriculum tasks required students to work toward complex learning outcomes involving comprehension and analysis of information. Four of the twenty-four lessons fell in this category. In two of these four lessons, the goals were to prepare an essay describing six heroes of the black race. This product or learning outcome was preceded by a cooperative learning activity in which students had reading materials available. In preparing the essay describing the six persons, students had a resource in the form of an essay outline of the criteria, with six sections of the essay provided by the teacher. The sections of the outline included the following: introduction; brief history of the person; contribution to society; achievements; people's views and conclusions (students' views). In this task students had to read and comprehend, explain to other members of the group, analyse and synthesize in order to answer the sections of the outline. These students were provided not only with the reading materials on the heroes but also an outline which helped them to organize their thoughts for the task. In the other two lessons, cases were written on the chalkboard and students were asked questions about these cases. They had to work individually to solve the problems posed in the cases. The product or learning outcome was to provide solutions to problems. In these four lessons, the learning goals as expressed in the product or outcome were complex and students had to engage in fairly high level thinking processes.

Why did teachers at Hillview High focus on the first category of tasks in which there was little interaction with teacher or text and where students engaged in low levels of thinking? The focus on low levels of thinking skills is not uncommon in classrooms (Doyle 1992; McNeil 1986). There are powerful forces within classrooms that shape curriculum tasks. Teaching is easier when it is routinized and becomes familiar to students, and when the flow of activities is smooth and almost predictable. It is easier to routinize tasks when learning outcomes emphasize lower levels of thinking. When the task content is more complex and the outcomes are more unpredictable, for example when the task is problem-centred, then classroom activities take much longer and make more demands on the teacher. It is partly for these reasons that one sees so few opportunities for divergent or higher-order thinking in classrooms. But in the case of 9X, the absence of instructional materials and textbooks also acted as a potent force in shaping the pedagogy, the classroom tasks and hence the kinds of cognitive activity in which students engaged. The shortage of teaching materials at Hillview High School and other upgraded high schools is implicated in the quality of teaching that takes place in those schools.

Reading and Learning

In some of the lessons where students had a text, they were required to read aloud because, as one teacher explained to them, "You read, but you are not understanding what you read. So we have to spend time on that." She was not the only teacher who required students to read aloud. Some students had difficulty decoding some of the words. As students read, the teacher corrected their pronunciation. Because of limited sight vocabulary and low word recognition skills, some students had to sound out some of the words they encountered in the text. Roughly one-half of the students – mostly the boys – read haltingly, using decoding skills. When such situations occurred, and students had to focus on their decoding skills, they often missed the meaning of some parts of the text and so missed the overall meaning of a passage. Students' inability to read fluently lowered their access to knowledge and understanding in the classroom where there was an emphasis on the textbook and on reading.

It was because of the prevalence of reading difficulties among students that the school made an effort to address this problem by hiring a specialist reading teacher. She admitted that the main reading problem which students experienced was word recognition. As she explained

> [Word recognition skills are] a problem for most of them because they have to decode these words. They have to use phonetics to figure out the word. Their sight vocabulary is very limited. And also for those who can read, comprehension is a problem. After they have read, you can't ask them any questions because they don't understand it.

Despite their problems of reading, however, many students who experienced this difficulty were reluctant to consult with the reading teacher after school because, in the view of the specialist reading teacher, such consultation was seen as a stigma that reflected poorly on them.

Most teachers acknowledged that 9X students had difficulty comprehending what they read. In the public performance of reading in class, their poor word recognition skills were quite evident. Since reading or listening to reading was the main student activity in about one-half of the lessons observed, how did students manage to do all the comprehension and interpretive tasks? An observation of one student in a lesson taught by a student teacher provides some clues. In this lesson on consumers and credit, students had the use of a textbook, which they were required to read sentence by sentence, with clarifications given for terms as appropriate. The language of the text was appropriate for a grade 9 class, and the book itself was published by a reputable textbook publisher who employs well respected writers with subject matter and pedagogical expertise. Nevertheless there were several words in the text that seemed to be unfamiliar to some students, which affected their understanding. Those students who were fluent in reading did not have this problem of gaining meaning. The sotto voce responses of a few students to the teacher's questions indicated that they understood the passage or that they had previous knowledge of the topic. For example, in discussing mortgages in this lesson, the teacher asked: "What is a mortgage?" Merle responded sotto voce almost in a bored tone of voice, "A loan, basically." The teacher wrote on the chalkboard, not hearing what Merle said, "A mortgage is a form of credit – used to buy a house or piece of land."

The following extract is a section of this lesson, taken from my field notes.

> The next passage is about credit cards. Students are asked to read. I am sitting beside Romero and I ask him if he knows what a credit card is. He says, "Yes."
>
> There are several words in the passage which I think need clarification, such as credit, credit history, and financial institution. But these words are not explained.
>
> I ask Romero if he knows what a credit history is. He says "No." The teacher has now continued to bank loans and students are asked to read the following passage:
>
> > Payment for credit is called interest which is calculated as a percentage of the money owed. Usually it is calculated as a rate per annum, so 46 per cent per annum means for every $100 owed for a year, the borrower pays $46 interest. If he/she borrows the money for six months only, $23

per $100 is paid. The sum borrowed is called the *principal*. There are also additional bank charges for servicing the loan.

There are two ways of paying interest. In one way, called "add on", the interest is calculated for the agreed period of the loan and then added to the principal. For example, interest on $10,000 for three years at 46 per cent per annum is $13,800. The borrower then arranges to pay the total sum of $23,800 in equal monthly installments. This kind of arrangement is suitable for persons who earn a monthly salary.

I ask Romero how they calculated the figure $23,800. He considers the question but he does not answer. The teacher does not explain this process.

There are other words used in the passage such as agricultural credit bank, commercial bank and collateral. I ask Romero if he knows what collateral is. He does not know. I build on what was read earlier about the borrower's income and say, "Suppose you go to the bank and get a loan and then you lose your job, what would happen?

He responds, "You don't get the money?"

I continue, "Well the bank would have lent you the money already. But now you lose your job, how would the bank be able to get back the money they lent you?"

He thinks but does not answer.

I explain, "That is the reason why the bank wants to know that you have more than your income – possessions such as a car or a house."

Students are continuing to read. There are other terms such as productive enterprises, expensive form of credit, and generate profit which need explanation, but students are simply asked to read.

(Field notes, 13 November 2003)

In this extract, we see an example of a lesson where the emphasis is on reading and comprehending as the main mental operation in learning. But some students, because of their limited vocabulary and sight word recognition skills, had difficulty in comprehending because they have to spend time decoding words. The teacher focused on reading as the main learning activity without spending much time ensuring that what was read was understood. Reading and comprehension may be easy for students with high reading abilities and comprehension skills, but not for those who do not have these skills, or who have difficulty in processing information. Since this was not a reading class, the teacher was not able to spend a great deal of time addressing the reading problems of some students at the expense of others. So those students who had these reading difficulties gained only a partial understanding of the text.

The extract also illustrates the ways in which prior knowledge of concepts can influence student learning and understanding, and how its absence can impede it. If these students had a social background within which these words had meaning or if they had knowledge of how banks operate, and how loans are procured and managed, maybe most of them would have been familiar with these terms. They would have been able to build on these concepts to create meaning from this reading. But many of these students did not have this background knowledge; the words in the text could not be related to their or their parents' lived reality.

Of course, not all students can have some prior knowledge of the concepts in the curriculum. Teachers are expected to teach in such a way that students develop an understanding of the concepts. They are expected to design lessons that allow this to happen. Relying on presenting the text as written does not ensure this understanding. As many researchers of teaching have pointed out, teaching for deep understanding of subject matter has to go beyond the transmission or delivery of subject matter knowledge. It requires competence in organizing this knowledge, in designing teaching/learning activities that allow students to engage with that knowledge and to work toward learning outcomes. It requires knowledge of subject specific approaches to teaching or pedagogical content knowledge. These activities that are required for teaching for understanding presuppose that the teacher has or can elicit knowledge of students' conceptions and use that in teaching. Teachers have to view the subject matter through the eyes of the learners (Shulman 1986; Talbert, McLaughlin and Rowan 1993).

This approach to teaching allows the teacher to represent the knowledge to students in ways that allow them to make connections with their existing knowledge or experience. Teaching students from a working-class background presents many challenges, since the teacher has to be familiar with their experiences or the knowledge they possess so that these connections can be made. Tharp et al. explain:

> Students' developing understanding builds on two foundations: new aca-
> demic material presented by the school and what they bring to academic
> topics in terms of everyday experience and knowledge. Effective teaching
> requires that teachers seek out and include the contexts of students' experi-
> ences and their local communities' points of view and situate new academic
> learning in that context. (2000, 26)

And so the problem extends beyond reading and listening. What is being
read is critical. This is where the teacher's imagination and ability to create
cases and other narratives that create vicarious experience can bring alien
subject matter closer to students' understanding. In this way, students can
construct their own meaning of the concepts instead of memorizing and
recalling what is written in the text. In lessons, such as the one in the
extract above, students had to rely on their listening and comprehension
abilities in the absence of activities that allowed them to construct meaning
by engaging with instructional materials, with the ideas of the teacher or
their peers, and with instructional stimuli that convey the meaning of concepts. In this case, the lesson reduced students' understanding of subject
matter, which in turn reduced students' access to knowledge and learning.
The extract also illustrates the lack of individualization or differentiated
instruction when the focus is on the delivery mode, reading and listening
to the written text.

How Teachers Determine Curriculum and Teaching Tasks

How did teachers determine teaching tasks – the core component of curriculum and pedagogy? Teachers were asked about their lesson planning and what considerations were uppermost in their minds when they
planned their lessons. Five of the six teachers focused on the students'
ability level. As one teacher explained, "I know that they [students in 9X]
are different, so I would not approach it in the same way as the others."
Another explained by contrasting the work done by 9X with the highest
streamed class:

> Well, you plan according to their level. You try to reach them as much as
> possible. When I'm teaching 9A [the highest level streamed class], I give
> them discussion work. When I go to 9X, I give them work according to what

they can manage. For example, if I'm doing fractions, I do a higher-level fractions [in 9A], and when I go to 9X, I give them . . . simpler work because I don't want to frustrate them.

So in planning curriculum tasks for these students, teachers chose content level that accorded with what they perceived students' academic ability to be.

Students in 9X were at different levels of ability, judging by the range of scores obtained in their examinations from their first year at Hillview High School, and based on teachers' own accounts of students' ability and potential. When teachers planned tasks without taking differences in student ability into account, it decreased some students' access to knowledge. During interviews with teachers, some responses to questions on lesson planning suggest that some teachers reduced the level of complexity of the subject matter when it came to teaching 9X. There is some evidence that teachers plan with an ideal or a composite student with a particular ability level in mind. That ability level is generalized to all the students in that class (Nespor 1987; Doyle 1992). This approach ignores students' individual differences. Since meaning and student learning inhere in the match between what students know or can do and what is made available for learning, some students may not get that meaning, and as a consequence they learn less than others.

Of the six teachers, one teacher had the students' reading problems uppermost in her mind. She felt that it was necessary to get these students who had reading problems to read. As she explained: "Although it's not to be done, because it is not a reading class, to get them to know the story, I tend to do more reading. In that class, I let them read or I read so that you can get them to do the work." One teacher indicated that she prepared only a content outline. This was a teacher who recognized the importance of planning challenging learning opportunities for students. Nevertheless, she only planned the content outline because she did not have to do otherwise. As she explained in the interview,

For me, at the start of the term, I always plan and am organized. By the end of the term, I start being lax, because it is not a situation where I know supervisors are coming to assess me. So I just go with the flow – just [go] to class and talk because I know I can . . . I read my lesson and I can just go and talk to the students. So it's a thing where I fall into a rut.

It appeared also that when the subject matter is simplified it is in turn associated with a type of pedagogy which emphasizes drill work, seatwork and low levels of thinking. Or teachers might have the perception that students in 9X could not handle higher levels of cognitive work or did not wish to be engaged in such challenging activities. Mr Stewart, the principal, concerned about student learning and the prevailing methods used suggested to teachers at Hillview High that they use more challenging tasks and instructionally stimulating materials. "Students need more. They need pictures. They need challenge. They are accustomed to TV and so are not able to listen to too much talk." This was said to some teachers and heads of department. The teachers with whom he spoke, however, disagreed. Students, in their view, did not want any of that.

It appears that most teachers believed that low-ability students could not manage discussion work or higher levels of thinking. As a consequence, they focused on basic skills and low-level thinking which has been shown to be alienating to many students. Teachers had in mind one particular level of ability when planning for teaching 9X. Since these students were not high academic performers, teachers chose content that was at a lower level of difficulty, avoiding teaching methods that required discussion and expression of their ideas.

At the same time, teachers were conscious of the few students in the class who, as they said, "had a lot of potential" and who were capable of much more challenging work. They made reference to several individuals whom they felt should be in a higher stream rather than in 9X. Some of them deserved to be in 9A. These teachers had even made representations on behalf of these students to have them transferred to a higher stream. Yet, they were unable to or did not take differentiated ability into account in their planning.

Teaching in 9X: "Just Giving Them Some Information"

Aspects of the pedagogy that was typically used in room 9X were evident in the curricular tasks described earlier. When we examine these tasks, and especially the task form of academic work, it is impossible to ignore issues of pedagogy. As Doyle (1983, 1992) asserts, the concept of curriculum task makes curriculum and pedagogy linked. The cognitive activity embedded in the tasks also indicates the kind of learning experienced by the student.

The heavy reliance on the written or spoken word for explaining concepts meant that students often failed to grasp complex ideas. Ability to explain subject matter so that students understand was one of the students' expectations of teachers. It also determined students' assessment of the teacher's ability to teach. One group of boys felt that roughly one-half of the teachers explained concepts well. This girl's comments reflected a positive view of teachers' explanations (the following quotations are taken from interviews with students): "Yes they teach well. They will sit down, most of them will explain it to us if we don't understand." But other students emphasized teachers' inability to explain.

He don't explain anything. He can't teach.

Ms ———. She doesn't explain. She just give notes and make it hard to understand.

Some of the teachers just write on the board and don't explain. And then when it comes to exam, you don't understand.

Like Mr D——, he's no longer at the school. He doesn't explain and if you say you don't understand, he doesn't answer you or he will say, "What is there not to understand?"

Some students had learned that their questions were not always welcome and, in fact, were discouraged from posing questions. Many students felt that teachers did not want them to ask questions in class. In some cases, students were scolded, insulted, embarrassed or "shamed" by the teacher when they posed questions. This is what a group of girls had to say about posing question in class:

Sometimes they are teaching and you don't understand what they are saying and if you raise your hand . . . and you're trying to get their attention . . . they say you are interrupting the class.

They sometimes say offensive things like, "I already explain it to you and I not going over it. I'm going to explain it one time and if you don't understand it, don't come to me."

When you try to ask them anything they shame you. They call you idiot.

Hyacinth L. Evans (HLE): What happens when you don't understand?

Students: Some of them go on hype. They say they not going over it. They don't know what you a go do.

HLE: Julien, do you ever ask [for additional explanation]?

Julien: Yes, miss. But the attitude of the teacher just turn me off.

Such responses on the part of some teachers had an effect on students when they did not understand what was taught. In interpreting the experiences of these students, it must be recalled that reliance on the written and the spoken word meant that students often failed to grasp the main ideas. So they had an even greater need and justification to ask questions of clarification, since they often failed to understand.

HLE: What happens when you don't understand something in class? What do you do?

Sherry: Sometimes I ask the teacher. Some of them shame you. I just sit down there and I look over my work, and sometimes I understand it more, but then sometimes I really don't understand it. Clueless. . . . One teacher I go to is Ms _____ and the ———— teacher and Mr ————. If you don't understand something he don't shame you, he try to explain. If you get something wrong, he go over. Even the next day he come back to it first.

Like the ———— teacher, if you have a problem in the class and you want to ask her about it, you don't ask, because you know she will shame you.

If you ask him something, him shout "Student [using angry voice], you are not paying attention. Pay attention!"

These students' reluctance stemmed from their assessments of teachers' attitudes and the sentiments behind the words and the tone of voice. It all depended on the teacher and the "vibes" that students received, and most teachers did not give the right "vibes". There were only a few teachers with whom students felt comfortable asking questions about subject matter. As these students explained, their painful experiences in the past had made them realize that question asking was not recommended.

You don't feel comfortable around them. You don't want to be near them. They don't treat you like somebody. They shout at you. They call you idiot and tell you you don't have any sense. . . .

Sometimes I would ask. But sometimes the vibes not right.

Ironically, teachers reported that they relied on students' questions to indicate what should be repeated, or they asked the students if they understood. If students said they understood, then that was an indication that all was well. What became clear was that students' regard for the teacher influenced their liking of the subject and their willingness to ask questions of clarification. Teachers on the other hand seemed unaware of these sentiments held by students.

To address this problem of understanding, students relied on the peers who understood or they relied on the notes taken in class. A very small number of students had relatives who were able to provide support in clarifying ideas or helping with homework, so they asked these questions at home. But for the majority, they did not have this resource. So students had difficulty with the dominant model of teaching, experienced difficulty understanding the material, and yet were unable to pose questions to the teacher because of fear of shame and embarrassment. Students came to rely on their own resources, such as their peers who understood and could explain to them, and on a few teachers who showed that they were willing to review and to go over concepts that were not clear to students.

This reliance on peers and family members was not sufficient to help students to master the curriculum, for they expressed the need for extra tutoring. Some students had in fact taken extra lessons elsewhere and had found this useful. Others, however, still hoped for extra help after school, and they communicated expectations of teachers which went beyond the usual requirements:

I think the school should have extra lessons or Saturday classes.

They can stay behind and help you.

I know all the teachers are supposed to help and to offer help but they don't do that.

I know that if I have a problem with a subject and I go to the teacher, if the teacher doesn't have time, the teacher will tell me. And if they have time they will help me.

Despite the logic of these students' sentiments, it was usually difficult for teachers to provide additional help for students. One teacher expressed the dilemma she constantly faced with decisions such as these, placing it in the context of teaching students with mixed abilities in a class that is large. She often recognized that one or more students needed help on a particular topic, but because of her teaching load and the number of classes and students taught, she might not follow up, might not even remember until she met the class the next time.

> You can see the size of the class – it's large. . . . So sometimes I don't even pick up on the student who is not following. The only time I will pick up on that student is on the test . . . when you see the scores and you say, okay, this one seems to be having a problem . . . but by the time I leave 9X, by the time I get to another class, I would have completely forgotten. Even if I had written it down . . .

Use of Students' Experiences

One consequence of the model of teaching described above was the limited use of students' ideas and experiences. Even in those lessons where there was some discussion of the text, students were often asked to recall and state the information in the text, not to use their experiences to construct an understanding of the concepts being learned. Their opinions on the topic were usually discouraged. And in the lessons observed they were rarely or never asked to use their imagination to conjure up a situation of their choosing. The pedagogy left little room for interaction between teacher and students. Students' participation was mainly reading from the text or writing what was written on the chalkboard or answering questions posed by the teacher. Since students had little opportunity to use their experiences in the learning of subject matter, they were unable to develop a deep, flexible understanding of it which would allow them to interrogate, analyse and critique the material, explain it in their own words and apply it to novel situations. These outcomes are possible when students have had a chance to reflect on the subject matter and apply it to new situations or to their own experiences and to what they already know. Unfortunately, the pedagogy limited the depth of the curriculum and the understanding gained therefrom. In the lessons observed, students ended up with a textbook understanding based mainly on memorization of the text.

Students who had no other access to subject matter knowledge other than what was presented to them, came to rely on the notes that teachers provided verbally or written on the chalkboard. This became their main source of knowledge. They reviewed these notes at home even when they had some difficulty understanding what had been taught. During lessons, students often seemed genuinely disappointed when notes were not given. The notes, even more than the textbook, were seen as valuable and critical for their learning. They reviewed and revised the content of these notes in preparation for their tests and examinations.

The Teacher-Student Relationship

Various teachers were seen to establish different types of relationships with students. The two teachers who used a more interactive approach to teaching, posing questions on the text and using examples while teaching were the teachers whom students mentioned as being approachable and encouraging. Nearly all the other teachers who used the traditional chalk and talk approach were seen by students as being emotionally and professionally distant. In some lessons, this style of teaching could be described as authoritarian and even punitive. Communication was usually given in the form of orders uttered in a stern voice, and infractions were quickly punished. This is illustrated in the following accounts of lessons observed:

> There is already some chatting and moving when the teacher enters. Students are crowded around her and they leave with a sheet. She is now giving instructions which I cannot hear because of the noise.

> Teacher: I'm saying this for the last time. . . . I am waiting. Put away all your bags now. If I see your bags on the desk, you go outside now. You [pointing to a boy] . . . out! Young man, please leave my class.

> Teacher begins to give instruction to the students. Information is related to ____. She walks around with hands at her back. She says to a boy "Young man, leave." He smiles as he leaves.

> Teacher: If you are not writing, please leave my class.

> (Field notes, 13 January 2004)

In another lesson, the teacher seemed reluctant to communicate verbally with students. Everything was written on the chalkboard – even instructions about what students were expected to know for an upcoming exam. When he had finished, this teacher took up his bag to leave without saying anything to the class – not even goodbye. As he approached me sitting at the back of the classroom, he said, as if to explain his behaviour, "This is not a regular class. I am just giving them some information." This pedagogy did not require much interaction between teacher and students and, in fact, it was observed that many teachers did not know the names of students.

Students picked up on these attitudes. The relationship influenced students' perception of the teachers' regard for them as individuals. Students believed that most of the teachers did not care for them. Since one of their expectations of teachers was for them to care for and encourage them, students reacted negatively to such attitudes and behaviour, and came to rely on those few teachers who showed that they cared about them and their future. A teacher's caring or not caring for students also influenced students' liking for and efforts made in the subject. This is what one student had to say:

> Some of the teachers I don't really like because they have an attitude. When they have an attitude, it seem that they don't like you. Most of the teachers they make the students not like the subject they teach because, for example, in ———, I know I can do better, but how she talk to us, it look like she just doing it because she has to, not because she want to. And we want her to want to . . . I don't want her to feel that way . . .

While this quote refers to only some of the teachers in this study, it reflects a relationship that was evident in most of the lessons observed. The transmission model of teaching limits the interaction between teacher and student to presenting or writing information, asking questions on the text, monitoring students' work and providing feedback. It did not entail much interaction or give and take. So, the model of teaching influenced the type of relationship that was established with the students. The two teachers who used the question and answer recitation format, which required more interaction, were seen by students as being more caring and encouraging.

However, this attitude toward the students could be specific to these students and not reflective of teachers' attitudes to all students at Hillview High School. Class 9X had a reputation for disruptive behaviour. Teachers were challenged to maintain an academic focus, maintain discipline, and manage behaviour. Although, as we shall see, disruptiveness was usually created as a result of a teacher's action or inaction, most teachers were unaware of the effects of their actions on students' behaviour. They associated this particular class with disruptiveness and lack of attention. Teachers described students as "restless, rebellious, unsettled, in need of attention, angry, a bundle of energy, and lacking in maturity". They had come to expect this disruptiveness in class 9X. And some teachers had experienced more than disruptiveness from some of these students. One student reported thus: "Sometimes, when the teacher is talking to the students . . . the students don't [show] any manners to the teacher. Some of them will tell the teacher bad words. . . . Some of them will tell the teacher what they are going to do."

So the teachers' regard for these students can be seen as a defensive move to prevent disruptions that may be brewing in the minds of students. Or it may be that some teachers had had enough of disruptive behaviour from one group of students. Teachers' responses to these students were thus constructed based in part on their previous experiences with them.

Discipline and Punishment

The model of teaching used with 9X placed the teacher in a position of power and control. The knowledge to be learned was dispensed by the teacher or read from books at the discretion of the teacher, with monitoring and corrections carried out by the teacher. To those who spend time in classrooms, this is a very familiar scenario. Teachers must establish and maintain control, and students must play their role by listening, being attentive, answering questions and recording information in notebooks. As a result, the teacher – the person in authority and the one who has the responsibility for what transpires in that classroom – has to ensure that students play the requisite role. In doing so, the teachers of 9X had to remind students of the rules of the game and, at times, to punish those who committed infractions such as speaking out of turn, being noisy, leaving their seats and so on. Since students in 9X found it difficult to remain still and be quiet during the many periods of down time when students were not actively or intellectually engaged, the act of teaching in 9X was often interspersed with the teacher's efforts to remind students of these rules, or to punish those who violated the rules. The teacher often had to interrupt himself or herself to tell the class "Quiet", "I said be quiet", "Shut up", "Did I hear someone talking?"

In addition to maintaining the control necessary to adhere to the teacher centred delivery model of teaching, many of the teachers observed used punitive and controlling practices to get students to behave. Students were insulted, demeaned, sent out of the class for simple infractions such as not having their books or not looking at the correct page. Students were punished for the following infractions: chatting, walking out of the class and not doing the work. Students related several occasions where they were demeaned and punished for slight infractions.

> Like the ——— teacher, we are afraid to ask a question because she shame us in her class. Like if you don't have on the school crest, she just say you can't come in her class. She doesn't care if you can't afford the crest.

> Sometimes, we don't have no book, and like some teachers will make us shame. She run us out. The reason why I don't have my book is normally because my mother, she can't afford it.

In some situations, the students themselves were also asked to make a note of peers who carried out these infractions. These peers would later receive some form of punishment. The following report was prepared by a student who was put in charge of monitoring students during the teacher's absence. The initials on the left refer to students who committed an infraction and who were being reported for punishment by the teacher.

> K—— speaking to D——
> JD—— calling Foody bi——
> DB—— not doing anything and talking
> KC—— not writing notes and chatting
> J—— speaking loudly
> R—— cursing in class

S—— cursing with R——
M—— outside when the teacher is teaching in class
R—— throwing paper in class
SB—— talking loudly in class
DC—— walked out of the teacher's class
NC—— outside walking up and down
JE—— walked out of the class

For this particular class, and maybe for other grade 9 classes, teachers found it necessary to monitor students' behaviour to ensure that they did not violate school rules and regulations and that they comported themselves in a way compatible with the model of teaching. In order to remind students of the need for orderliness and adherence to classroom rules, most teachers spent time at the start of the lesson on little bits of protocol designed to get students in a state of readiness for the lesson, and to remind them of the rules for behaviour. During this time, teachers would inspect students' attire, monitor their ability to be silent while standing, and examine the neatness and arrangement of desks and chairs. In one lesson, the teacher began the academic part of the lesson after more than forty minutes were spent on rules, appropriate behaviour, chiding students and electing monitors. This was an extreme case, however, and such preliminaries were usually dispensed with in less than five minutes.

Students reported several other instances where punishment was meted out to students by teachers or by the specialist teacher in charge of discipline. The protocol often created resentment or annoyance among students, sentiments sometimes made obvious by body language or even actual responses. Students considered it smart to disguise their feelings since they recognized that the heavy hand of the school authority could easily descend on them. But some students showed their disagreement with policies in a variety of ways – by being dilatory, refusing to carry out orders, simply walking away or remaining silent when they were expected to respond. Such behaviours created occasions for teacher-student confrontation and punishment. In some situations, students responded to the teachers' behaviour in unexpected ways. This got them into trouble as seen in this report by a student: "She likes to shout at us and act as if we are adults and she argue with us and when we argue back at her, she punish us."

Confrontations between teachers and students were also a result of student infractions which could escalate into a physical confrontation as a student relates below:

> C —— was doing the sums and just because the classes are boring and we need a little fun in the class, he was kind of trying to let it be fun. So, meanwhile, he is doing the sum on the board and he is joking. . . . [Then] Mr —— came in and just because some of the boys at the back were talking and he was telling them to shut up, C—— didn't shut up. So he got angry and C—— was at the board laughing and making noise. Mr —— go and lick the boy. I don't think he should have done that. I don't think a teacher should lick a student so severe.

However, the confrontation can lead to harsher and more punitive results for the students even though they may recognize the infraction:

> There was an incident where the teacher and D—— were talking and the teacher came up to him. Now D—— went up to the board and got it wrong, and the teacher use the ruler and it's like he didn't mean to hit him in the face but on the shoulder. And he hit him again, and the boy get mad and grab the ruler from him and drape him up and the teacher drape him up back and lick him against the wall. . . . The boy said he won't bother with it, because he get suspension already and he don't want get kick [expelled].

In some cases, the punishment had a direct effect on students' grades as seen in the case where students were not allowed to take a test because they were absent when the topic was discussed in class, or when a student received a low grade because the teacher lost his paper. There were many instances of teacher-student confrontations which resulted in suspensions or students being asked to leave the room for the remainder of the day. These experiences were related by students with much emotion and anger, because they saw such practices as unfair and unjust. Such incidents also resulted in lost learning time.

Students also chafed at the bits of protocol that they endured, which appeared irritating to many students who referred to them as "foolishness", and they expressed anger at the harsh punishment received. This affected the way they felt about the teacher. Harsh disciplinary practices created resentment, and affected the teacher-student relationship and the level of trust that developed. Students felt that the infraction rarely warranted the severity of the punishment.

Students' Responses to Teaching and to Punishment

In some lessons, it was clear that students were engaged in the activity, were focused and paying attention; in many others, however, they showed that they were uninvolved and uninterested by not paying attention, sleeping, or paying attention to other matters. One could sometimes hear the hissing of teeth or whispered comments as they were obliged to do something that did not seem appealing or to make sense. The tedium of writing information from the chalkboard was often annoying to some students as in this reaction by O'Neill:

> (Students have been writing notes from the chalkboard for some time.)
> O'Neill says, "Why they never put this on the book list, mek mi haffi write all a dis." He says this in a weary, frustrated, maybe angry tone of voice but he continues to write. There is much hissing of teeth by many students.

In some lessons there was evidently a subtext of students escaping from the lesson. Students would find a way to be excused by the teacher. In this incident below, when the teacher had spent an inordinate amount of time drawing a diagram on the chalkboard, Nadine managed to get an excuse to leave the classroom. As she left, with a broad smile on her face, one student at the back said, "Nadine, you get wey."

Students had their own views on the teaching methods used by most teachers.

> Some of them just come in and write notes on the board and go wey.

> I don't like ———. You just sit down and write off notes.
> It's kinda hard; pure notes, and when exams come around and you have to study, you panic because you can't remember nothing. . . .

> Some of the teachers just write on the board and don't explain. And then, when it comes to exam, you don't understand. And when you try to ask them anything them shame you. They call you idiot. . . .

> When she come to class, it's pure notes. She doesn't explain anything. . . .
> In science class, now, if we had the experiments, the class would be much more fun and we would understand the notes.

I'll tell you the truth. In —————, the teacher was just writing notes on the board. She just writing, writing, so I just left and went to Mr Lawrence's class.

In these comments on teaching, students are indicating that teachers did not teach for real understanding, that the pedagogy did not allow them to understand and therefore to recall easily, that the method was lacking in interest, and they were not learning. Yet, there were many occasions when students were intellectually engaged and focused on their work. Most teachers acknowledged that the students – or most of them – could do their work. Furthermore, there were several occasions at the beginning of a lesson when students were alert, ready to learn and paying attention. All students became focused on their academic work when they were assigned tasks that required them to think, to figure things out and to seek out solutions to problems. On such occasions, students were usually quiet and focused as they wrote what was written on the chalkboard in their notebooks. Such attention usually occurred after the students had discussed a topic that they found stimulating. Sometimes their interest in a lesson resulted in animated discussions, with the level of noise comfortable and not loud. Such discussions and a low level of chatter indicated interest and involvement.

The Construction of Classroom Disruptiveness

Although students believed that the cause of these continuing episodes of student disruptions and inappropriate behaviours rested with their fellow students (and at times with themselves), an examination of field notes of lessons revealed that such behaviours occurred primarily when certain situations existed in the classroom. The origins of disruptive behaviour did not always rest with individual students and their propensity to talk, to act out or to liven up the class. There were many situations where students were focused and academically engaged, and interested in what was being taught. Disruptive behaviour resulted from a series of events having to do with teacher actions or inactions, poor use of time, the technology of teaching and pedagogy. Examples of a teacher's inaction or action is when the teacher is late for the class or absent from the class for a short period of time, or when the teacher uses time unproductively during teaching. In the latter model, students worked individually on seatwork and the teacher corrected students' work individually. In these situations, the teacher was unable to give attention to all students at the same time, and so there were many periods of down time or "dead time" in the classroom when students were not productively engaged. These periods of down time encouraged some students to begin to chat among themselves, to play, to relieve the boredom in any way possible and, even in some cases, to leave the class. Very often when they left the class, they would assemble outside the classroom door, which added to the noise level in 9X and the adjoining classrooms.

Disruptions also occurred during transitions between timetabled periods. Although they were not timetabled, these short transitions occurred between scheduled classes, and they allowed students to prepare for the upcoming period. However, on many occasions the teacher was late – sometimes up to forty minutes late. On those occasions, students would begin to talk among themselves, tell jokes and generally to engage in idle chatter. It was very often from such, almost innocent, beginnings that students' disruptive behaviour began. Students chatted and played while waiting. On many occasions, when students began to talk among themselves, to play and to move about, it was not always easy to refocus their attention. The following three extracts are examples of the effect of teacher lateness on student behaviour and on the classroom culture.

Case 1

| 12:20 p.m. | I arrive during the silence period that comes after lunch. I enter the classroom and wait for the teacher. The noise level slowly rises. Students come and go. |
| 12:38 p.m. | The teacher comes to let students know that she will soon be there. I ask J what happens when a teacher is late. Does anyone inform the office? He says, "No, not usually. Sometimes when they are very late, we just sit and wait." |

Case 2

| 9:42 a.m. | (The class should have begun at 9:10 a.m.) Students are chatting among themselves. The noise level slowly rises. |

| 9:42 a.m. | The teacher arrives and approaches the chalkboard. |
| | Students continue to chat among themselves as if she is not there. She writes on the chalkboard. |

Case 3

9:20 a.m.	After the teacher of English leaves, students wait for the teacher of the next class. They talk quietly. A student explains that they have to wait for the teacher who takes them to the lab.
9:27 a.m.	About six students leave the class.
9:41 a.m.	About one-half the students have now left the room. A girl goes to the chalkboard and writes [name of subject] October 16, 2003. The noise level rises.
9:45 a.m.	The teacher arrives.

(Field notes, 16 October 2003)

These accounts reveal the dynamics of down time that resulted from teacher lateness. Students began to talk and to leave the classroom, and the noise level rose. The absence of an authority figure in the classroom gave students the opening to socialize and attend to non-academic matters. At times, the teacher found it difficult to change the tone of the class and to get students to focus on academic work. After such incidences, it did not take long for the act of talking and "livening up" the class to become the norm in class 9X. Such non-productive use of time, and such behaviours on the part of students began to assume an air of normalcy.

Down time, which often led to engagement in disruptive behaviour, was also the result of the model of teaching. When students performed a task, the outcomes of the tasks had to be communicated to the teacher or to other students after which, feedback would be provided. Since students worked individually on seatwork in most lessons observed in 9X, the teacher had to do some monitoring of seatwork to ensure that each student understood what was to be done and were engaged in completing the task. Thus, in many lessons observed, a good portion of the lesson was devoted to the monitoring and marking of seatwork. This is illustrated below:

(This class was preceded by a mathematics class.)

9:50 a.m.	Some students have left during the transition and have not returned. Students are chatting among themselves.
9:51 a.m.	The teacher enters. Students stand then sit on her entry. She sits at her table. Nothing is said for about two minutes. Finally, the teacher says, "When you're quiet, I'll start." Students become quiet.
9:52 a.m.	Teacher hands out [marked] exam paper. She remains at her desk and calls out names of students who, one by one, go to get their paper. (This continues for about twelve minutes.)
10:10 a.m.	Teacher begins to write the answers to the test on the chalkboard.
10:20 a.m.	Teacher sits at her desk, and begins to speak to individual students about their exam performance. No task is set for the other students. Students begin to talk among themselves.
10:25 a.m.	Teacher now takes the register. Students still not assigned a task.
10:30 a.m.	End of class.

(Field notes, 12 January 2004)

This example of a class that focused on revision of an examination reflects the kind of marking of seatwork that requires the teacher to give individual attention to a student while the others are assigned nothing to do. This led to many periods of down time as the teacher engaged with one student.

There were other occasions where teachers were observed to write or draw on the chalkboard for more than half an hour while students wrote the material in their notebooks. During this time, with little interaction between teacher and students, it may happen that some students are not interested in writing the material, or do not have an overall sense of the meaning of what was being written. So students would begin to talk among themselves. A conversation with a neighbour that began as a question seeking clarification on the task, or as a comment on what was happening in the classroom would soon turn to non-academic matters and thus become a different kind of conversation. Additionally, the kind of teaching/learning activity to which they were subjected often became the butt of jokes among students. The following excerpts from field notes illustrate the effect of a teaching model in which there was little interaction between teachers and students or among students where the teacher spent a great deal of time writing on the chalkboard, as well as on monitoring and correcting seatwork.

	(Students have been given a task to complete the blanks in sentences. These sentences were written by the teacher on the chalkboard.)
9:55 a.m.	Teacher comes to the back of the room, leans against the wall and reads silently from a book.
10:05 a.m.	First student takes up his work. Teacher looks at it.
10:10 a.m.	Teacher goes to her seat and looks outside. Students begin to chat among themselves.
10:14 a.m.	Boys to the left of the room discreetly throw paper planes to one another.
10:15 a.m.	Teacher begins to monitor students, walking down the aisle between rows of desks. There is a girl asleep. The teacher wakes her. She touches a boy, urging him to finish. Some students are playing as the teacher corrects a girl's work.
10:16 a.m.	The noise level rises and the teacher gestures to students to calm down. But there is no change in the noise level. The teacher continues to correct individual work.
10:20 a.m.	The teacher now stands erect and looks at the class. She appears ready to work on the chalkboard, correcting the exercise with the entire class. (One half hour has passed since the students started filling in the blanks.)
10:21 a.m.	Students begin to shout out the answers.
10:25 a.m.	The teacher has now completed the blanks in the ten sentences. She stands and waits. The students continue their own business, talking among themselves, throwing paper planes.
	The teacher says, "Okay?"

10:26 a.m.	A boy erases the chalkboard. The teacher writes another set of ten exercises on the chalkboard.

(Field notes, 8 October 2003)

The teacher spent a great deal of time writing an exercise on the chalkboard, while students waited for this activity to be completed. Students began working on the exercise only after the writing was finished. This teacher also spent time doing individual monitoring and waiting for students to complete the exercise. Those who had completed their assignment often yielded to the temptation to chat and play. It did not take long for the attention of students to be distracted and for the noise level to rise. This was a language lesson in which the goal was to allow students to use the language. Yet the method – especially the teacher's writing on the chalkboard for more than ten minutes at a time – reduced the opportunity for teacher-student interaction, and for students to use the language. It also encouraged students' inattention and disruptiveness which in turn reduced students' ability to engage with the curriculum.

In situations like these, whether there was seatwork to be monitored or corrected or not, the construction of disruptiveness followed a pattern. When the teacher was speaking to an individual student, the other students were not engaged. The unengaged students began to talk among themselves. The noise level would then begin to rise. Having experienced this sequence of activities during teaching events on several occasions, students began to regard this kind of classroom activity and their chatting and disruptive behaviour as normal. In such situations, some even concluded that a focus on academic behaviour was abnormal, as one student remarked of A—— who was always observed reading or focused on his work, regardless of what was happening in the classroom. "We call them nerds. Like A——, always with his head in his book no matter what is going on."

Students reported that there were other reasons why they behaved in ways that disrupted the class. Their level of respect for the teacher had much to do with their behaviour, as these students explained:

In Ms ——— class and [with] the ——— teacher, they don't make any noise. But with Ms ———, they speak when they like, and they get on her nerves. It's only a few teachers that they like. They don't give trouble with them.

If the teacher come in and you don't have the right vibes, you'll talk. Or if they feel the teacher won't punish them, the teacher is very soft, they will talk.

If the teacher is soft, they just walk out when they ready. You see, they know nothing will happen so they don't really care.

Classroom disruptions had an impact on student learning according to students' reports. Disruptions prevented them from paying attention, listening and concentrating, and could even make them leave the class. These are what students had to say.

Sometimes it is our fault why we don't get a better education, because we idle sometimes, and we don't listen to the teacher who try to explain to us.

Sometimes when the teacher talk miss, they don't listen to the teacher. They just walk out of the class while the teacher is teaching. They just do what they want to do.

Sometimes you are trying to listen and other students are disrupting.

They disrupt the class when others are trying to do their work.

When students in class are trying to make a point these [disruptive] students don't give them a chance.

These students acknowledged that the disruptive behaviour of some students – estimated by one teacher to be about one-half of the students in 9X – interfered with their engagement with the curriculum and consequently with learning. Students could miss what was being explained, or be unable to concentrate on the matter at hand, and to reflect on what was being taught. Or some students might leave the class and thus not be present to participate in the lesson. In all these ways students' disruptive behaviour had an impact on other students' engagement with the curriculum.

When asked their views of class 9X, teachers referred to their classroom behaviour and the reasons for this behaviour. They also referred to their academic potential. All teachers who were interviewed or with whom I spoke informally agreed that there were some students in 9X who had the potential for academic achievement. Some of these students were prevented from achieving their best for various reasons having to do with the peer group culture, with some individual need, or their domestic situation. So teachers recognized students' innate potential. But, in their view, this potential was not easily realized because of the many challenges that they had to face.

The students have potential. The only problem is that they talk a lot. But there are students there that if you take time with them, sit with them, you can get the work done.

There are some there who will do the work. If you tell them to do this, they will do it. There are others who need some attention.

9X have potential. There are some of them who want to learn but because of the destructive behaviour of other students, they tend not to learn.

These three teachers focused on students' academic potential and the reasons why they were not performing at their level. They could see the students' ability although results did not always reflect it. However, these teachers were in the minority. As we saw earlier, teachers when asked to describe the students in 9X, emphasized their disruptive behaviour in the classroom. They attributed this behaviour to the social environment from which students came, the physical condition of the classroom or the social composition of the class. But it was clear that teachers placed emphasis on students' background or the social environment in which they lived to explain the restlessness and disruptive behaviour, as seen in the following comments by four teachers:

I think that's because of their social background. Most of them are from the same style of community.

It could be family problems. It could be the physical classroom itself. The noise is all around them and everyone is misbehaving.

They are rebellious. It could be family problems; it could be the physical classroom itself.

They could do better if they were more settled. And it's not just settled at school but at home, because most of the time students come to class and they are trying to understand and because of the situations at home, they are not able to really concentrate on school.

Thus, when teachers thought of 9X they thought primarily of their disruptive and inappropriate behaviour. They recognized that some students had academic ability or potential but that they faced great odds in realizing that potential. They attributed the disruptiveness and restlessness of students mainly to their social background and to the communities in which they lived and secondarily to factors within the school, factors over which they as teachers exercised some control. Of all the teachers interviewed, only one teacher cited the curriculum and the pedagogy as contributing factors to students' restlessness.

Teacher Caring and Encouragement

One of the expectations that students had for teachers was for them to care for students and provide encouragement when needed. This encouragement was given by only a minority of teachers and there was a consensus among students as to who these teachers were. There was Ms Kirlew who was firm and fair, and who provided the encouragement they needed. There was Ms Carey who often reminded them of the sacrifices that were being made for them and their need to persevere and do well.

> Like Mr Lawrence and Ms Kirlew, they really push us. They're the only teachers who see the good in us, who believe in us, and they have a little respect for us. The older teachers, they first want to judge us according to what they have heard about us from long time. I'm not saying some students don't deserve it because some of them are bad but they need to give us motivation. They have to encourage [us].

> Like Ms Carey, she will tell us that if we don't take our studies seriously we're going to regret it. We're going to be like beggars on the street selling bag juice. And you don't want to be like them.

Reminding students of the sacrifices being made on their behalf or the terrible fate that would befall them if they did not succeed academically or at least try their best was one frequent way in which these teachers tried to encourage students. There were quite a few teachers, however, who by word and deed made students believe that they did not care for them as individuals.

> Some of the teachers . . . say they don't really care if you learn, as long as they get their money. . . . They say as long as they get their pay, they can just sit down and watch us fail, for they already get an education and now they have a job.

> Some of them will tell you "You're dunce and good for nothing." I don't think a teacher should do that.

Some students believed that teachers, rather than berating them for their poor academic performance, should understand their situation and the many "issues" with which they are faced. The teacher, they felt, must begin to assume additional responsibilities, given the reality of the social life of students. One student commented that "teachers should try to get the students to cooperate because when the students look at the teacher and the teacher just talking, some of the times their head in space. [They] need to find those students, connect with them."

Mr Lawrence is a teacher with whom all students in 9X had a very special relationship. He is about thirty years old and had had previous experience teaching part-time at a technical high school. He joined Hillview High School a month before the study began and this was his first experience as a form teacher. In the formal interview, and in several informal conversations during the first year of the research, he communicated his special love for the students and his interest in their welfare. He knew details of their personal and domestic lives and the problems that each individual was facing. Referring to them as his boys and his girls, he clearly wanted them to succeed, especially those whom he knew had great potential. As he said:

> Some of them can excel. But because of the class they are in, they have no way for somebody to push them. For example J—— and K—— in 9A, if you were to put Andrew with those boys, he would soar higher than what he is doing now. . . . And it is not just Andrew, there is Julien, and Sean and some others . . .

Mr Lawrence was not embarrassed to state that he loved his boys and girls, and cared about them. He was always there to intervene when they got in trouble with teachers and other adults at Hillview High School. For him, "teaching is innate. I always wanted to be a teacher." He recognized that, as teachers, they were dealing with adolescents who had problems, and for this reason, what was important to him as a teacher was the all-round development of the students. As he said to the students on many occasions, he was able to empathize with them, because he also came from a humble background. On many occasions during form time, he described the sacrifices that his mother had made for him to succeed. Nevertheless, he was realistic enough to know what the students in 9X were capable of doing and he always expressed concern about their behaviour and welfare in and out of school.

Parents and students alike recognized the special relationship that he had established with the students, and they in turn demonstrated their high regard for him. Students knew his telephone number by heart as I learned one morning when, in a desperate effort to find him, I asked one of the students where he was. Mr Lawrence had the telephone numbers of all parents and would call them regularly, even when there was no problem. Mr Lawrence said of parents: "If I scold a child now and send them home, they would say nothing. Because they say I'm the only teacher that calls them."

Students in 9X without exception held him in high esteem. To them, he represented the parent or trusted friend that they wanted in their teachers and needed in their lives. He was the adult who showed love and caring, who encouraged them when they needed it and who recognized that they were adolescents with problems. For the boys especially he was like an uncle or big brother, and the regard and the need were such that many boys admitted that they would stay behind after school and after the sports which he coached, so that they could talk with him about their personal affairs.

> I think Mr Lawrence has turned into a parent. If we don't do well, he gets on our case. . . . He really cares about what happens in our school work. And if the teacher isn't there, he comes and stays with us.

> (In response to a question about who is their favourite teacher.)
> Mr Lawrence. He knows how to talk to the students, even when he is disciplining us, he can find some kinda joke that we don't get too vexed. So we actually listen to him and respect him and he is our form teacher and he is there for us. It's actually like he is our friend; he talks to us like a friend. We appreciate it. He says when it comes to our school work, he's very serious because he knows we can do better; he's very serious about that.

> Mr Lawrence, he's the only teacher who will push us; he will sit down and talk to us like a parent; he puts a lot of confidence in us to have us believe in ourselves. He's really a great teacher. He tells us we can do better than we are doing, and we can try harder. He's a teacher who understands how to deal with children, especially our age group. To me that's really good.

> He tells us not to waste time. Because our mothers invest in us so that we can grow up and get a good job and take care of our parents.

Mr Lawrence therefore represented the ideal teacher that the students had described, expected and wanted. As they had said early in the research, they wanted teachers who, in addition to being good teachers, believed in and cared for them, encouraged and motivated them, and was someone in whom they could confide. They wanted someone whom they could respect and who would respect them. These qualities were especially important to those students who did not have a father or a mother in their lives. For many of those students, the parent who was present in the home was not emotionally available to them. With the many challenges or "issues" that these students faced, having an adult to whom they could relate at school was critical. There were two other teachers, Ms Carey and Ms Kirlew, who they said came close to according them the trust and respect they craved. They, like Mr Lawrence, did not follow the dominant model of teaching described earlier, and like Mr Lawrence, they showed encouragement and caring for students.

Chapter 5   Students' Voices

In this chapter, the students' comments on a range of issues related to self, school, family, learning, teaching and teachers are reported. The information in this chapter is based on the interviews held with students during the second and third terms of the first year, and the second year of the research.

The Students

Unlike most classes at Hillview High School, there were more boys (twenty-five) than girls (seventeen) in 9X. To some teachers, this ratio had a lot to do with the dynamics of the class and the classroom. They attributed the hyperactivity and restlessness that typified this class to the class size and gender ratio. More than 40 per cent of the students lived with two parents, either with a mother and father (24.3 per cent) or mother and stepfather (8.1 per cent) or father and stepmother (8.1 per cent). Nearly one-third of the students lived with their single mother. The others lived with a guardian (for example, an aunt, brother, sister, grandmother or friend). Roughly 90 per cent of parents worked at jobs that can be classified as service and shop workers, or elementary occupations as specified by the Jamaica Standard Occupational Classification (STATIN 1991). These two categories of work fall at the lower end of the occupational scale. Parents' jobs as reported by the students include dressmaker, attendant, salesperson, higgler, small shop owner, cashier, nurses aide, bartender, driver, security guard, janitor and domestic helper. A few parents were professionals: computer specialist, engineer and teacher. Most parents live in inner city areas of Kingston.

Some of these students were happy to come to school because of the amenities, attractions and benefits of school and also because the environment of the school was so different from their own communities. About 83 per cent of the students stated that they liked being in school most of the time, with only 16.2 per cent being undecided or disagreeing with the statement "I like being in school most of the time." A fairly high percentage (70.4 per cent) of these students felt good about themselves all or most of the time, 21.6 per cent said they felt this way sometimes and 8 per cent said they felt this way now and then or never. However, a disturbingly high percentage of students (30 per cent) felt that they did not belong in school or were undecided about the matter. The other 70 per cent of students agreed that they belonged in school most of the time. The majority of these students consider their education to be most important. Seventeen (46 per cent) of the thirty-seven students who completed the questionnaire stated that their education or passing their CXC examinations or staying in school was most important in their lives. Twenty-four per cent chose their parents (or their mother or father) as most important. Others felt that making a sports team, settling down academically, getting a job and money were most important in their lives.

Although most students felt good about themselves most or all of the time, there were, nevertheless, many things that they worried about. These worries had to do with schooling, examinations and finding a job later. Their greatest worry – which most students mentioned – had to do with passing their CXC examination, with thirty-one students (83.8 per cent) making mention of this. Almost 60 per cent worried that they would not be able to get a job later in life, a worry that reflected the current economic situation in Jamaica, and the importance to them and their families of having a job. This response may also reflect the experience of their families in finding or holding a job. Almost one-half of the students (45.9 per cent) worried about being able to go on to study after they had completed their CXC examinations. Other worries chosen less frequently were violence in their community (24.3 per cent) and being able to stay in school (21.6 per cent).

On a typical weekday, students engaged in the normal activities that young people their age usually engage in. Homework, studying or reviewing work completed in class took up much of their free time, as did doing household chores, watching television and engaging in sports or play. Twenty-eight students, or 78 per cent of those who completed the questionnaire, said that they did homework or reviewed classwork after school on weekdays and on the weekends. Another 38 per cent spent their time doing household chores and watching television. They also did training or some kind of sports, went to church, or to the library, hung out with friends, listened to music, read a book, slept or looked after siblings. Students, therefore, tried to balance the demands of school work with household chores, leisure activities and having fun.

The form teacher, Mr Lawrence, had many opportunities to talk with these students albeit with the boys more than the girls as he acted as an athletics coach and spent time with them after school. It was his view that many of his students were often angry in part because they had to assume adult responsibilities too early, responsibilities that included taking care of siblings. Others had different demands or were involved in adult-like relationships. Some were involved in sexual relationships. At least one girl relied on this relationship for her economic survival, and at least one of the students in 9X had been a student in an adolescent mothers' programme.[1] Many of these students had had to assume adult responsibilities at an early age. Some, according to Mr Lawrence, felt cheated because they were unable to take part in many of the activities that other students of their own age were able to enjoy.

The group interviews allowed students to air their views on a range of issues that were shaped in part by the questions that I posed. (See appendix 4 for a copy of the interview schedule.) Their responses are presented under the following headings: friends and peers, how students viewed themselves, issues that students faced, views of school and schooling, how boys and girls viewed each other.

Friends and Peers

When students began their day, they had made a physical and social transition from home to school. The majority of students came by bus from distant communities that were different from the middle-class community where Hillview is located. For most students, entering room 9X was an occasion to reconnect with friends, to catch up on events of the past twelve hours or so, to discuss personal matters and, for a few, to plan for the day's lessons, to plan for activities after school and to complete homework. During periods of transition between timetabled sessions, students were seen to chat and laugh with one another, to engage in friendly "sparring", to write poems or short cryptic statements on the chalkboard in reference to fellow students. These were moments of discretionary time for students, and they used it to engage in camaraderie and playful behaviour. For example, a boy would indicate by the movement of his hands that he wanted to play fight, though others might or might not be interested. Jokes were made at others' expense. It was especially during these periods of transition that one saw various personalities being expressed. They passed the time talking, joking, playing, throwing paper aeroplanes to one another, walking over to another's desk, and in various ways revealing the carefree attitude of adolescents. Some students quietly read a book or completed homework while this buzz of activity took place around them. Many of them adopted a relaxed posture, lounging on the straight-backed metal chairs, legs outstretched, perhaps with elbow on the desk and cheek resting on one hand. Very little of this activity was related to academic work.

These activities on the part of students represented the informal side of school, the friendship and peer culture that contribute significantly to a student's development.[2] This is the informal world of peer groups and special friends, which forms part of the social context that shapes the lives of boys and girls at school. This informal peer culture constituted one of the two learning contexts provided by the school outside of the academic curriculum. The other was the extra-curricular activities, which were described in chapter 3. For students, being with their friends was an important part of school. It was one of the major attractions of school, along with their teachers and the subjects that they liked. For these reasons they liked coming to school. So friendships and the informal peer culture were important to students and were an important aspect of schooling. While students acknowledged their commitment to passing their examinations, and to getting an education, they also acknowledged that their peers were important to them. Their friends acted as a resource and a means of support, at times as a distraction, as a means of taking attention from the task at hand, and a relief from the boredom of lessons. Such instances of peers providing relief from boredom were observed several times over the period of the study and, as we have seen, students' propensity to allow themselves to be distracted depended on their interest in the lesson, or the subject matter or the efficacy of the pedagogy.

As a result of their proximity and close contact throughout the day, students in 9X, like students everywhere, developed a culture of their own, and a knowledge of each other's interests, quirks, abilities and preferences. This was made evident on several occasions throughout the study. For example, on one occasion, when a gift of a set of novels was being distributed, students who were given the responsibility to distribute the books showed that they knew which of their peers would be interested in a particular book. They would call out to a student and draw the attention of one of their peers to a particular book. On that occasion, Mr Lawrence, who was present, explained that they knew each other's reading preferences. The similarity in behaviour and values among groups of friends was evident in the cliques or friendship groups that existed in 9X. Most of these cliques were same sex groups but members of these same sex groupings admired and respected members of groups of the opposite sex as became clear when we discussed the admirable qualities of boys and girls in the class.

The differences in values and academic focus among students were quite evident. These differences were observed in class and were referred to by teachers and students alike. There were students who could be relied on for academic and emotional support. There were a few students who were known to be bright and willing to be helpful. Their peers relied on students such as these for academic support when they did not understand a concept discussed in class. Andrew, the highest achiever, who was regarded as helpful and well behaved, was one of those to whom students often went for explanations. The clique of which this boy was a member was also a well admired group of students. O'Neill, another member of this group, had been elected as a class representative. In the interviews, students referred to the members of this group and to two other groups as good students whom they admired.

On the other hand there were students who had a reputation for creating disruptions, being disrespectful and for not paying attention in class. These students – who were mostly boys – were described by their peers as disruptive, troublemakers, noise makers, disrespectful and vulgar, and frequently had confrontations with teachers. At times these students would "skull" or fail to attend a class and would even inform the teacher that they did not want to take that subject. These students were oblivious to what their peers said to them. The behaviour of these students was disliked by most of the students in 9X, as these students indicate: "The misbehaviour with some of the students in the class – they don't take telling from other students"; "They are disruptive. They don't spend time to pick up a book." Students such as those referred to here had a propensity to create distractions, to draw attention to themselves and to their behaviour. And while their behaviour was, in certain circumstances tolerated, it was often an unwelcome annoyance to those who preferred to concentrate on their academic work. These disruptive students regarded school as more of a social than an academic setting. The other students learned to live with them.

How Students Viewed Themselves

Students in form 9X entered Hillview High in 2001 with satisfactory performance on the GSAT, and with average levels of passes in various subjects: 70.3 per cent in mathematics, 72.3 per cent in science, 76.8 per cent in language arts and 77.3 per cent in social studies. They came from primary schools where they had been good students and had performed well. When they spoke about themselves, they viewed themselves as bright students.

They held high expectations for themselves. One could say they had a high academic self-concept.

> Yes, I think I'm very bright and intelligent. [Susan, a very confident self-assured girl.]

> Yes a whole heap of students are bright, Miss.

> Miss, when you check it out, some of them can do really, really well. Some of them could do better than all the other rest of the class. For example, Martin got a low grade. If he put out a bit more effort he could do well.

> I believe everyone in the class is bright because if you don't study, you won't do anything on the exam, and that is the major problem with these students.

The third and fourth students above distinguished between ability and achievement or results. They acknowledged that some classmates were bright but they did not all work hard. Others echoed this sentiment: "Most of them are bright but they waste time"; "When it comes to our work, we do it. We're serious. But sometimes we idle." A few students placed more emphasis on hard work than on ability. This student came twentieth in the December examinations. "I wouldn't say I am bright but I can do better. I didn't put out enough effort. I need to settle down, concentrate more on my work and watch less TV." The students interviewed represented all levels of achievement while in form 9X. They felt that their achievement depended on hard work, and they felt that working hard was important to success. But as we will see later, they also recognized that there were many constraints within the school and within the classroom that militated against their success as students.

Students placed a high value on education, as was shown earlier. For some, education was important because they saw it as a way of escaping their current situation. For others, it was what their parents emphasized as being important. And for others, it was important for their future and for the careers that they had already chosen for themselves. Andrew saw education as a way of escaping the fate that others his age had already succumbed to: "On the road, I see some idlers and I wonder what they are going to be in the future. I wouldn't like to be like them . . . so that pushes me a lot to do my work."

Students also made a link between their own education and their future quality of life. As O'Neill said: "Sometimes I think that if I don't do well, when people get old how are they going to live? So that's why I have to do well from now so that I can take care of my family."

Thus, most students liked coming to school and placed a high value on education. Passing their examinations was the most important thing in their lives and also something that they worried about constantly. For the most part, they thought very highly of themselves and of their academic ability. According to their reports, they spent their time like typical adolescents their age, dividing the available time between studying, socializing with friends, listening to music and having fun. However, there was a minority of students who did not feel that they fitted in at school.

Issues That Students Faced

Most of the students came to school with issues on their minds. Although these issues were never discussed publicly, teachers and students seemed to know that they existed, and what they were. Teachers made mention of them in passing when discussing the behaviour or performance of students. Students mentioned these issues in reference to other students. But they were obviously reluctant to discuss these specific problems that other students faced. Guidance counsellors mentioned the term "issues" several times in our discussion and gave examples of the problems and challenges that students faced at home. One issue that was mentioned by all – students, teachers and guidance counsellors – was that of students' low self-esteem, although its specific nature was never elaborated on. As one guidance counsellor expressed it, "We have a lot of children who are suffering from low self-esteem. You hear them expressing that they want to get this or that . . . and a lot of them are concerned about their looks. And they'll be looking in the mirror several times during the day."

Another issue that students were not so reluctant to discuss was the financial difficulties that they faced. In the words of one girl, referring to the "situation" faced at home and school, "sometimes it's financial because they don't have financial support so they keep thinking about it". Another girl, without being specific, referred to the range of issues faced by her and her peers which she felt teachers should take into account: "They should know that we are growing; we have school pressure, we have home pressure, we are under a lot of pressure. We have peer pressure every day. They need to understand that when we come to school, we are still under pressure."

Students' financial difficulties often led to friction between teachers and students. Teachers often seemed exasperated with students when they did not have the proper materials, or were unable to bring books and materials to class. Students' comments showed that they perceived their teachers to be lacking in understanding regarding their financial position:

> Most of the teachers think your mother and father have money. I'm not sure if that's what they think, but they act like that. It's not everybody have money.

Students also felt that teachers should show some understanding since they knew that their parents "don't have it". In one lesson, most students in a class were sent out of the classroom because they had not bought the graph paper needed for a test. The result was that they were unable to take the test. When I spoke with the students about this incident, they expressed anger at the teacher who, they felt, should understand that some of them could not afford to purchase this material. Some parents, however, did try their best to procure books and other materials for their children even though they had financial difficulties. According to Molly, "My mother doesn't have it, but she knows I'm interested in literature and those things, so she try to find the money because she knows it is important to me."

Students' financial difficulties were also apparent when they had to plan for class outings, and in general discussions about life at school. Lack of money seemed to be a fact of life for these students and it affected many aspects of school life. But although financial difficulties posed a constant problem, students could make light of their financial situation. For example, in one discussion in which the students and the form teacher Mr Lawrence were planning a class trip, students were asked to make suggestions regarding places of interest that they could visit, bearing in mind the cost. One student said Disneyland, another suggested Boscobel, and another suggested a hotel. They were clearly having fun and their financial difficulty in finding the cost for the trip was transformed into something to laugh about. The financial difficulties were made evident in the number of students needing lunch or bus fare, a need the school made efforts to address.

Another problem that some students faced was friction with parents. Their relationships with their parents was often a bone of contention, according to one girl. "Sometimes it's parents – what they do and say. They [the students] feel left out; sometimes they feel rejected. . . . Sometimes they feel hurt and they start acting a way and they are not speaking to you, and you wonder what is the matter." In their view, issues at home could influence learning. "It's not just settled at school but at home because most of the time, students come to class and they are trying to understand and because of the situation at home, they are not able to concentrate on school."

Like most high school students in Jamaica, the family situation of many of these students was unstable. Only one-fourth of students lived with their biological mother and father and one-third lived with a single mother. Many parents had migrated to other countries, leaving their young children behind, usually with a grandmother but also with aunts and friends. Since most of the parents worked at blue-collar, low-skilled jobs which often had long hours, it can be surmised that parents were not always emotionally available for these adolescents (Brown 2001). Troubled relationships with parents or substitute parents were one of the problems that students discussed most frequently with guidance counsellors. As one of these counsellors explained, "They have a lot of problems of relationships with parents. A lot of the students who come here, when you investigate their backgrounds, you find the parents are having a warm time with them at home. So, sometimes all of that spills over into the school."

Students were not inured to the problems that existed in their communities. One guidance counsellor stated that many students had experienced violence or the effects of violence within their midst and the school, in some cases, had had to provide grief counselling for some students who had lost a loved one. Some fathers were in prison. While adults spoke about these issues with me as researcher, students themselves were reluctant to discuss them although they often hinted at them. These issues or "situations" or problems may be among the matters that some students wanted to confide to teachers. As a result of the harsh conditions of life in most of the communities in which students live, they themselves had developed a harshness in their interpersonal relations. It was very common in their communities to respond to disagreements with anger or to fight, and some students displayed the same aggressiveness at school. A few had been found carrying knives at school. Other issues or problems that students typically faced included relationships with the opposite sex. Relationships with members of the opposite sex are normal for boys and girls at this age.

While many students discussed these matters with the guidance counsellors, others refrained from doing so because they were unsure of confidentiality. Instead, they discussed their problems with a few of their peers whom they trusted and respected and who were good listeners. Students rarely found it possible to discuss their issues with their teachers. Most teachers were not able to establish that type of relationship with them, and teachers' schedules did not allow for this type of interaction. Teachers themselves complained of being too busy even to attend to the instructional needs of students. The only teacher in whom students could confide was their form teacher.

Views of School and Schooling

As we saw, most students liked to come to Hillview High School for various reasons, such as the location of the school, the ability to be with friends, the subjects they were learning and the future possibilities that schooling offered. One girl described her views thus:

> I like coming to school. I like just looking forward to a new day. I like learning new things. I love the subjects, well most of them – like social studies and Spanish. We learn a lot about our country, about languages, some things that we have never heard about or even talked about before . . . just coming to school will help us to learn and talk more about it.

But this enthusiastic feeling about school was not experienced by students all the time. There were times when school itself affected their will to learn even though they wanted to learn. One student said, "Sometimes when you come to school, you just feel lazy because it's not exciting. You really want to learn. But sometimes . . . it's boring and the teachers are not exciting. They don't teach exciting things."

It was this combination of a pedagogy lacking in interest and teachers who were unapproachable that sometimes made school an unexciting place for students, despite their desire to learn and despite the value they placed on education. Students were very selective about the teachers whom they admired or with whom they had a good, trusting relationship. They referred to Ms Carey, Ms Kirlew and Mr Lawrence as persons whom they liked and trusted. Some teachers definitely had positive qualities that students liked or admired. Some teachers were encouraging or supportive. As this boy indicated, "many of the teachers want to see us strive, to come to something". When it came to other teachers, however, all students felt that they could not engage them in discussions about curricular or personal questions.

How Boys and Girls Viewed Each Other

Students in 9X had had at least nine years of co-ed schooling. They shared classroom space, talked, joked, teased, argued and even fought during lunch breaks and recess, and for the most part, they cooperated on matters academic and personal, working and learning together, in a spirit of helpfulness. In these various interactions, boys and girls had the opportunity to evaluate themselves in relation to their peers and the opposite sex. This self-appraisal process is critical for adolescents who are forming images of themselves and developing norms for appropriate behaviour as informed by peers. They had the opportunity to consider the self in the context of gender roles.[3]

Students had an opportunity to share their views about boys and girls during the group interviews. In so doing, they revealed not only their impressions of their male and female peers, formed after nearly three years together, but the gender messages received from the school itself and the wider society. Students were asked the following questions:

What makes a boy/girl popular?

What do you think of boys/girls who are studious and work hard?

Do you behave or talk differently when boys/girls are in the conversation? What is different? Why?

Do you think the teachers are easier on the girls than on the boys?

There were some similarities in the characteristics and behaviours that students thought made boys and girls popular. But there were some striking differences. The similarities had to do with human personal qualities such as being a person others can relate to or being a person who relates well to others. The first – being a person to whom others can relate – was mentioned more frequently with respect to girls (five responses) than to boys (three). The following are characteristics that students attributed to popular girls:

Someone you can relate to. Nice person.

Someone you can sit and talk with.

They are fun to be around.

Fun to be with, jocular, will greet you.

Someone you can trust. Someone real cool.

However, students attributed different characteristics to popular boys. Their responses reflected different notions of what was feminine and what was masculine. Boys who were popular were expected to excel in sports (five responses), do their school work/get high marks in school work (four responses), have a lot of girls (four responses), be able to rap with the girls (three responses), or be able to dress well or be neat (three responses).

Sports

In sports. If you come first in all you races. It gives you a little exposure to the whole school.

Sports. You become well known.

Active in sports.

Participating in sports activities and participating in class.

He plays a sport and he is handsome and neat and dresses [well].

Connection to Girls

The number of girlfriends you have.

Can rap with the girls. The girls like you. You have a lot of girls to come look for you in the class.

The girls like you.

They are handsome and the girls are hazy [crazy, wild] about them.

Dress

He can dress.

He looks neat.

Academic Work

If you do your work, others respect you.

Participation in class.

How you do your school work.

You get high marks in school.

It was also important for boys to participate in class. However, a boy would not necessarily be popular on the basis of any one of these characteristics. As John explained, in reference to boys' popularity, "everything is important; everything adds up". And each characteristic was given different degrees of salience by different students.

In contrast to the boys, physical appearance played a key role in determining a girl's popularity, although that by itself was not enough. Girls who were popular had good looks or a good shape or were stylish, in addition to having the personal qualities mentioned earlier. In most cases, all three were cited by the same person or group.

Stylish

Hot hair style. Hot clothes. Have a boyfriend (said by girls).

Someone intelligent; carries herself well; does a lot of activities (said by girls).

Her personality. A person you can talk and relate to. Somebody beautiful, because some people just think of what is outside. Somebody who is neat and who you can sit and talk to (said by girls).

Have a good shape (said by boys).

Put on make-up. The way she acts. Like they are more mature (said by boys).

She looks good. She has great shape. How she acts. She knows how to talk with people (said by boys).

With the emphasis on physical looks and personal and interpersonal qualities, there seemed to be more of a consensus on what was important for girls than there was for boys. At the same time, both boys and girls mentioned a range of other qualities that were important for girls – a range that was not evident when they spoke of the popularity of boys. These additional characteristics, mentioned by only one person, were: personality, intelligence, not loud and interruptive, bearing, being good in sports, being rich, working hard and participating in a lot of activities.

When we examine all the responses made in relation to girls' popularity we see that personal qualities were more frequently mentioned and were given more salience than the others relating to physical appearance. Personal and interpersonal qualities were important to both boys and girls, but girls elaborated on this idea and gave examples of such girls in their class. For example, this personal quality was discussed in relation to S——, who was seen by some girls as easy to talk with and trustworthy.

> Like S——, she's a pretty cool girl. She is like a friend you really can talk to. You can go to her with anything and you're real and comfortable round her. She's real cool in class, I feel comfortable with her. She and I are not really friends but you can trust her.

It was interesting that, although students mentioned boys' participation in class as a basis for their popularity, they did not mention this for girls. One group of students agreed that "almost all the girls pay attention in class", and so this was not seen as a special characteristic that would make a girl stand out. At the same time, boys who paid attention to their books all the time and lacked some or all of the other qualities, were considered "nerds". They were usually respected for their academic focus but not admired.

> HLE: What about boys who focus and pay attention and do their work all the time?
>
> Girls: We call them nerds – like ——, always with his head in his book.
>
> HLE: And the girls – if they are focused and do their work all the time?
>
> Girls: Most of the girls are like that.

Some nerds, however, can be very helpful to students, willing to explain something that is not grasped by others. For those students, "they are not popular but you admire them".

Thus, apart from the personal and interpersonal qualities, which appeared to be important for popularity for both sexes, there were gender differences in what students thought was important for being liked and being popular. Excellence in sports and relations with the opposite sex were critical for boys to be liked, but not for girls. This was the opinion of both sexes. On the other hand, physical appearance was important for girls to be popular, but not for boys. The interpersonal qualities that were important for both sexes were more emphasized for girls than for boys. There was more of a consensus on what was important for boys' popularity than for girls' popularity, as both sexes mentioned a wide range of characteristics, qualities and behaviours when referring to the popularity of girls. What emerged in these responses were girls' and boys' definition of masculinity and femininity and the ways in which they were constructed in the everyday life of the school.

Boys and girls usually socialized in same sex groups during break, lunch and after school. However, they also got together and conversed, argued and joked around in mixed groups. When boys and girls were together in a social situation, their conversation covered the gamut of topics. As one girl expressed it:

> Most of the time, we talk about boys. And we talk about life, what we want to do when we grow up, we talk about the teachers. And when someone is stressed out, we try to make them forget the situation. Most of the time we just give jokes and play a lot.

Boys, however, admitted that in a mixed group the topic of conversation was different from what occurred with a group of boys. In most cases, the boys set the agenda. One group of girls said, "They always set it. So we talk about girls"; "Sometimes they just interrupt you. They don't say anything important but they come to want to find out." For the boys however, the topic of conversation depended on their feelings for the girl. As one boy said, "You put some lyrics to the girl. But if not, you act normal, you talk about the school subjects." Friendship therefore existed among girls, among boys and between girls and boys. This friendship and easy relationship was important for both sexes. As Molly said, "I feel real comfortable with the boys in my class. I can ask them anything."

The interviews also gave students a chance to reflect on gender and the image of the male and the female. Molly, Susan and Jean were discussing friendship and the easy relationship that the girls usually had with the boys in their class.

Molly: I said to them the other day, "Guys you have it easy right?" And they ask, "What you mean?" And I said, "You don't have any pain." And [one] said, "What you mean guys have it easy?" And I said, "Trust me, guys have it easy."

HLE: Do you think they have it easy?

Students: Of course! [Laughter.] Guys are really lucky.

HLE: So what makes them lucky? They don't have monthly pains. What else?

Susan: In primary schools, they have it much easier to get in than we.

Molly: They can have a conversation with a girl without tripping up. They can joke around and stuff.

HLE: So they can approach a girl but you can't approach a boy. Is that it?

Susan: No we can't.

HLE: So that makes it easier for them?

Molly: Yes. And in some places, the woman still get down graded.

HLE: Down graded meaning what?

Students: Women are seen as inferior to men. They are to be the second, not to be equal.

HLE: You have experienced that. But do you think that?

Molly: Sometimes I feel that way, because . . .

HLE: There's a difference here. You think you are inferior and you know that they treat you as if you are inferior.

Susan: I don't feel inferior. But they want you to feel inferior.

HLE: What about you Jean [who has been quiet]. Do you think boys have it better?

Jean: Of course.

HLE: And what we're talking about is how they [teachers] treat girls.

Jean: They treat boys better. In the church too.

The conversation above shows the girls have begun to experience what it means to live in a patriarchal society.

Boys and girls were asked whether teachers were easier on the boys than on the girls. There was no consensus on this matter: boys and girls disagreed among themselves. In citing reasons why the teachers were harder on the boys, both boys and girls referred to the boys' need for academic monitoring and their usual misbehaviour. In the interview, all students were asked the question: Do you think the teachers are harder on the boys than the girls? This was their response:

Girl: Yes. I think so because the boys need more attention than the girls because the girls don't give a lot of trouble as boys.

HLE: So the teachers pay more attention to them because of that?

Girl: Yes and that's okay with me.

HLE: It doesn't make the girls annoyed?

Girl: No. No not really.

Girl: No, they go down on the boys because some of them are just lazy. Most teachers pressure the boys [more] than the girls because the boys idle. The girls are more focused.

HLE: So they get on the boys' case but not on yours because it is not necessary to do that with you.

Girl: Yes.

This boy, who thought that girls were treated better than boys, nevertheless cited the misbehaviour of boys to justify the teachers' stance: "I think that they treat the girls a little easier than the boys. Probably the boys give a little more trouble so they have to be harder on the boys. They have to take drastic measures with the boys."

The subject matter may also have much to do with the participation of the boys or the girls and consequently with the teacher's stance toward the boys or the girls.

Boy: Ms Carey . . . . She thinks the boys participate more than the girls.

HLE: Really. So they treat the boys better than the girls?

Boy: Yes, sometimes – certain teachers. And it depends on the subject. Like in Home and Family, the girls are better at that, and in Technical Drawing the boys are better. It depends.

So while there is disagreement on the question of gender differences in teachers' treatment of students, both boys and girls cited the problems that boys had or had created for themselves (such as being lazy, needing more attention, being unmotivated) to explain the fact that teachers paid more attention to boys – whether the focus was on instruction or behaviour.

Notes

1. Adolescent sexuality and preoccupation with their sexuality are normal aspects of adolescent development (Feldman and Elliott 1993). Sexuality refers to individuals' sexual attitudes, practices, identity and desires. It should therefore be distinguished from gender, which is a social construction of the role and status of males and females in a society. There is more information on male than on female adolescent sexuality. Research on adolescent sexuality in Jamaica indicates that young people, on average, engage in sex at a relatively young age. A regional survey of adolescents attending school, carried out by PAHO/WHO in 1996, indicated that 37.7 per cent of this group had had sexual intercourse. Of this number, almost 50 per cent had had sex by age ten or younger. The Jamaica Adolescent Study also indicated that younger adolescents aged eleven to fourteen are likely to be initiated into sexual activity, with boys (64 per cent) more likely than girls (6 per cent) to do so (Eggleston, Jackson and Hunter 1999). The onset of sexual initiation in Jamaica is the earliest in the world (World Bank 2003, xiv). What is more disturbing is the fact that more than 40 per cent of the adolescents in the PAHO/WHO study reported that their first sexual encounter was forced.

Adolescent boys appear to have adopted the values of the dominant culture which states that, for the Jamaican male, sexual prowess is the ideal, having multiple partners is a badge of honour and a basis of respect from other males, siring children is a sign of manhood, and that the male should be dominant in the male-female relationship. Furthermore, a man is not a real man unless he is sexually active (Chevannes 1993; Kempadoo 2003). Although the younger adolescents in the 1996 study by Eggleston, Jackson and Hunter did not approve of sexual activity among children their age (they felt that one should wait until they are twenty-one or twenty-two years of age), nevertheless, a sizeable proportion of the boys felt that they should and would engage in sex at their age (of eleven to fourteen). It appears from this study that young people experience some conflict between their mores and their actual or intended sexual behaviour. In other words, the boys felt that it was inevitable that they would engage in sex even if it was desirable that they would not. These conflicts and contradictions stem in part from the pressure that boys experience to engage in early sex. Not engaging in sex may make them appear to be chicken or not to be a man (Eggleston, Jackson and Hunter 1999).

While less is known or written about female sexuality, recent studies indicate that many adolescent girls regard sexual activity, but not necessarily pregnancy and childbirth, as important to being a woman. These more recent studies appear to disprove the notion that pregnancy and childbirth are a signal of womanhood (Eggleston, Jackson and Hunter 1999; Kempadoo 2003). While there is some evidence that many of these adolescent girls engage in sexual activity because of the pleasure they derive from it or because it is a sign of being a woman, there is also evidence that many engage in it because of economic necessity. Included in this number would be many students. Nevertheless, there are many young adolescents who do not engage in sexual activity. The reasons given for not doing so include fear of pregnancy, fear of HIV–AIDS and other sexually transmitted diseases, the fear of a loss of reputation among the girls, and the desire to wait until marriage (Eggleston, Jackson and Hunter 1999).

2. For many adolescents, the way in which they are seen by their peers is the most important aspect of their lives, and some adolescents will go along with anything, just to be included as a member of a peer group. Being excluded means stress, frustration and sadness. Today, adolescents spend an increasing amount time with their friends during and after school, and there are more facilities in urban centres such as the modern shopping mall where such gatherings can take place. Good peer relations are necessary for normal social development in adolescence. It is through peer relations, more so than in family relations, that the adolescent learns about symmetrical reciprocity in relations, the notion of fairness and justice and how to work through disagreements with peers, in order to become a part of a peer group. Adolescents also observe their peers' interests and ways of thinking and try to integrate all this into their own sense of self (Santrock 2004, 187).

Adolescence is also a time when the intimacy of close personal friendships assumes increased psychological importance. Such friendships provide playful companionship, support, affection, social acceptance and a basis for social comparison, thus contributing to adolescents' sense of well being and self-worth which shape their overall development. There is evidence that adolescents spend more time in meaningful interactions with close friends than they do with parents. This includes time spent at school. Adolescents use friends as a source of cognitive and social support. Best friends are there to listen, understand, share problems, and think through problems and solutions. Because such friendships are based on shared interests and have such emotional effect, friends usually share similar attitudes to school, and similar educational aspirations and achievement orientations. For these reasons, friendships and friendship networks are significant to students and their developing identity. It often happens that friendship groups or cliques are formed at school where adolescents meet on a regular basis. Such cliques may be based on friendships or involvement in common activities.

3. Because gender is a significant organizing principle in Jamaican society, it is an important factor in the lives of adolescents. There is now a body of research on gender socialization in the Caribbean which indicates that boys and girls have different socialization experiences at home and the early school years (Senior 1991; Leo-Rhynie 1997). By the time they reach adolescence, these differences in gender socialization manifest themselves in many ways. For example, there are gender differences in the number of hours spent on reading and doing homework, as well as in the careers that boys and girls would like to pursue. At school, as in other sectors of the society, adolescents become aware of the restrictions and opportunities that the society holds out for males and females. Femininity and masculinity have different meanings and refer to different behaviours on the part of males and females, and the violation of norms and expectations is harshly and swiftly dealt with.

One area in which boys and girls differ is the area of social relationships. There is evidence that boys and girls differ in their knowledge of and attunement to human relationships and concerns. Girls are more likely than boys to reveal detailed knowledge about human relationships that is based on listening to and watching what happens between people. It appears that girls can sensitively pick up different rhythms in relationships and follow different pathways of feelings. For this reason, females experience life and relationships differently from males (Gilligan 1982; Gilligan and Taylor 2004).

Chapter 6   The Construction of
                Academic Achievement

The students in 9X entered Hillview High School in 2001, having been assigned to the school on the basis of their performance on the GSAT and in part on the basis of parental choice of school. The GSAT comprises tests in four subjects – mathematics, science, social studies and language arts – and a test in communication tasks. Candidates with high levels of passes in each of the subjects in the GSAT are allocated to the schools of their choice, usually the traditional high schools that have an established reputation. Although there are now many upgraded high schools that have begun to show good results in the CXC examination, most of these schools are not regarded as schools of quality and are, therefore, not the first choice of students when parents make their application for the GSAT. Some students in form 9X, however, did choose Hillview High School as a first choice in their application.

Because of this system of student allocation to schools, most of those who attend Hillview High School did not score in the top quintile of each of the subjects in the GSAT. The GSAT passes were available for only 23 (55 per cent) of the students in form 9X. (The missing data may be a result of transfers to and from the school after September 2001.) The GSAT data show the following average levels of passes, and the percentage of students who gained these average levels of passes.

Table 1: GSAT Scores for 9X Students on Entry to Grade 7 (2001)

Subject	Average Grade (%)	Range	Points
Mathematics	71.5	58–83	
Language Arts	78.2	65–86	
Science	73.0	60–83	
Social Studies	78.7	65–90	
Communication Tasks			9.8 points out of a possible 12 points

The data in Table 1 show that, at entry to Hillview High School, students in form 9X were performing at a very satisfactory level in all the subjects tested at the GSAT level. Students were assigned to their grade 7 classes on the basis of their GSAT scores. However, because students admitted to any one school would have GSAT scores that fall within a band of scores (as seen in the ranges above), these results are typical of the performance of all the students who entered Hillview High School in 2001.

However, in the three years at Hillview High School, the performance of 9X students has deteriorated. It is true that the GSAT is nationally norm-referenced while the grades received at Hillview High are based on teacher-made tests and a specific curriculum. Nevertheless, the class averages also indicate some deterioration over time. In the grades reported below, the class average is calculated by summing all the average grades received by each student and dividing by the number of students in 9X. A student's average grade is calculated by summing all the grades received for each subject and dividing by the number of subjects. There are about fourteen subjects offered in each examination.

The following table presents the class averages and range of scores for the school-based examinations taken by students in 9X when they were in grades 7, 8 and 9.

Table 2: Class Averages and Ranges for 9X, 2001–2004

	DECEMBER 2001 (GRADE 7X)	JUNE 2002 (GRADE 7X)	JUNE 2003 (GRADE 8X)	JUNE 2004 (GRADE 9X)
Class Average (%)	49.7	49.7	43.15	38.90
Range of Grades	27.7–62.2	26.9–69.0	31–58	15.6–55.8

In the first school-based examination in December of 2001, the class average reflected a steep decrease in the level of students' performance compared with their GSAT scores. In the second school-based examination taken in June 2002, the class average and the range remained roughly the same as that obtained in December 2001. In their second year, when they were in grade 8X, there was a slight reduction in the average class grade, and the range had narrowed somewhat. However, the grades fell significantly in the June examinations when the students reached 9X. In addition to the general reduction in the average class grades, the wide range in the scores is also quite remarkable. This indicates that there is a wide range of academic abilities in this class. It indicates the need for special instructional arrangements, such as cooperative learning groups, special instruction to facilitate learning for some students, and the use of more active teaching methods.

The data obtained in this study provide some clues to some of the factors and conditions that contributed to this deterioration in average class grades in 9X. In thinking of the influences on learning and academic achievement, I take into account all that precedes learning within the context of the school, such as having the right environmental conditions for learning, paying attention during a lesson, engagement in learning tasks, being able to develop meaning and understanding of subject matter, having or developing an interest in the subject, and having misconceptions and contradictions explained. Such actions and conditions lead to or influence learning. The multiple ways in which each factor interacted with others to influence learning and academic achievement for the students in 9X in this school will also be discussed.

Environmental Features

Environmental features included the physical features and conditions of 9X, and the student peer culture, which influenced student behaviour and disruptiveness. The location and design of the classroom made the room always very hot despite the many windows and the presence of a fan. As a result, there was often a general lassitude and fatigue evident, especially in lessons immediately before and after lunch. These conditions reduced students' attention and ability or inclination to concentrate. A second environmental feature was the noise and disruptiveness so common in this classroom. These conditions often made it difficult for students to hear what the teacher was saying, to concentrate and to work in a focused way. They also affected students' ability to learn, as those who were creating the disruption were not listening to the teacher and the others could not be attuned to what was being said while there was "too much confusion". The disruptiveness that resulted from the student peer culture interfered with teaching, disrupted students' engagement with subject matter and with learning, and reduced teachers' expectations for the class as a whole, as well as their interest in the students. These direct results of the disruptiveness had secondary effects on teacher's planning and teaching as well as their interactions with individuals and groups of students in 9X.

Learning requires a proper environment that allows students and teachers to think and reflect, and engage with subject matter in meaningful ways, thus creating a climate for learning. The physical learning environment is only a precondition for learning. But without this prior condition, it is difficult to ensure that the curriculum is implemented and curricular objectives are met.

Structural Features

The significant structural feature of the school that influenced student achievement was the streaming of students, according to their academic ability, into different classes at the same grade level. Assumptions underlying streaming are that bright students' learning is likely to be slowed if they are placed in mixed ability groups; that slower students are likely to develop more positive attitudes about themselves and school if they do not have to compare themselves with the brighter students, and that teachers can accommodate individual differences more easily in homogeneous groups (Oakes 1985). Teachers' reports regarding the streaming of students at grade 7 are conflicting, and the person who had responsibility for assigning students was no longer at the school. One report was that there was no streaming until grade 8. Another report was that the students with the highest marks in English and mathematics at GSAT were assigned to 7A while all other students were randomly assigned to the other grade 7 classes. Since there was no agreement on the method of allocation in 2001, the GSAT scores were obtained for 9A students and compared with those of 9X. The GSAT results showed the following average levels of passes for 9A, based on 61.5 per cent of the students:

Mathematics
73.5 per cent of students (with a range of marks between 54 and 90)

Language Arts
77.6 per cent of students (with a range of 61 to 91)

Science
74.6 per cent of students (with a range of 63 to 83)

Social Studies
78.3 per cent of students (with a range of 69 to 93)

The average pass in the communication task was 9.8. When these results are compared with those obtained by 9X, there were only slight differences in the scores obtained by each class. Students in 9A gained on average 2 points more in mathematics, but scored 0.6 points less in language arts. The other grades were more or less comparable. This finding is not surprising, as students assigned to the school would have scored within a narrow band of scores. It can be concluded that, whatever the method of assignment in grade 7, students in 9A and 9X gained roughly similar grades in the GSAT. Most teachers agree that there was some streaming by the time students reached 8th grade, after they had

had the opportunity to demonstrate their academic ability, potential and other student qualities that influence teacher decisions regarding placement. At the end of grade 7, those who were achieving at a high level were assigned to grade 8A in September 2002. Students of 9X were, as a group, judged to be of average ability, being ranked fourth in the six classes on this grade level. So by the beginning of grade 8, there was streaming.

Streaming acted as a framework for different interpretations, self-evaluations and actions on the part of teachers and students. This occurred in various ways, such as teachers developing different expectations for the different grade 9 classes. In the case of 9X, most teachers developed lower expectations for students' academic work, their interest and commitment to learning. The reputation of the class was one factor that influenced teachers' evaluation and interpretation. Lowered expectations on the part of the teacher began a cycle of poor teaching methods, a relaxation of standards and rules for students' academic work, and unwillingness or reluctance to follow up or to provide additional help and tutoring.

Streamed classes appeared to have different cultures and different learning environments. This was evident after I observed a lesson taught to 9A, the class deemed the "brightest" among the six grade 9 classes. I observed an English lesson which was the same as that taught to 9X some days earlier, a lesson in which students worked cooperatively to do research on some black heroes. The criteria for the task were explained and students were expected to work on their own. The differences between the two classes were striking. Students in 9A were engaged and on task: they asked questions and had them answered, and the teacher stood by ready to respond to students' comments and questions. The classroom was quiet. This one observation and the comments of various teachers support the conclusion that students in both 9X and 9A were influenced by the peer culture of the class, that teachers had developed different expectations for students in these two classes, and that classroom learning environments differed by stream. The influence of the peer culture was cited by some of the students in 9X, who were concerned about their own learning:

You notice when they move out they start work harder.

Some of the students are not set back like we. All of a sudden N——
[a student who had been in 8X the previous year] was doing better in
eighth grade and they move him up. . . . We knew he could do his work
and now I think he's changed.

The learning ethos of a class may also be influenced by students'
adjustment of their own effort to match the level of the class. Some
students might feel constrained from working hard when placed in a
lower stream, because this went against the grain of the ethos of the
class. As Molly explained, "Everybody can do good. They can do it.
But if you go and do good, and *they* not doing good, everybody start
fight against you."

Given the differences in the class ethos and behaviour of grade 9X
and 9A, the average grades for students in 9X were compared with those
of students in 9A in order to compare the academic performance of these
two groups of students studying in two different learning environments.
The following table presents the class averages and range of scores for
the school-based examinations taken by students in 9A when they were in
grades 7, 8 and 9.

Table 3: Class Average and Ranges for Class 9A, 2001–2004

	DECEMBER 2001 (GRADE 7X)	JUNE 2002 (GRADE 7X)	JUNE 2003 (GRADE 8X)	JUNE 2004 (GRADE 9X)
Class Average (%)	60.76	60.58	59.67	61.22
Range of Grades	47.4–72.6°	42.4–71.3°	45.1–82.64	42.2–87

When we compare the performance of grade 9A with that of 9X shown
in Table 2, we see a marked difference in both the average scores and the
range of scores of the two classes. From the first school-based examination
in December 2001, when they were in grade 7A, students were performing
at a significantly higher level than the students in 9X. The average class
grade average was 11.06 points higher than that of grade 9X in December
2001 and 10.88 points higher at the end of the academic year in June

2002. By the end of the second academic year in June 2003, however, the point difference was 16.17, increasing to 22.32 by the end of grade 9 in June 2004. The difference in performance widened in the three years from grade 7 to grade 9.

Since the GSAT scores of these two groups of students were more or less similar, the differences in academic performance of these two groups can only be attributed to school level factors. Streaming can, therefore, be said to have influenced students' academic achievement in various and complex ways. In the case of 9X, the curriculum was adjusted in ways that simplified subject matter for some students without addressing the need for creating challenging learning opportunities for the majority. In addition, teachers of 9X adjusted their expectations to fit the ability level of the class. This adjustment was evident in their method of teaching, in their interactions with students and the expectations communicated to students. Teachers' expectations and their propensity to compare 9X with the "brighter" grade 9 classes were picked up by students and in turn influenced their self-perception. Expectations and self-perceptions were part of the dynamic that shaped the climate and the teacher-student relationship, although the effect on their learning and academic achievement could not be determined. Students in this class began with lower achievement levels in grade 8X, and this led to lowered expectations, altered students' self-perceptions and unwillingness on the part of teachers to go the extra mile for a class which, moreover, did not always behave in appropriate ways. The self-fulfilling prophecy was thus realized, and the very students who needed additional help, tutoring and encouragement as well as additional resources and materials for teaching, were the ones who received less.

Pedagogical Features

As described in earlier chapters, the pedagogy was based on the transmission model of teaching, with limited instructional materials or textbooks and limited engagement or interaction with the text in cases where the textbook was used. The focus of teaching was to pass on information by means of the spoken or written word. As a consequence of the absence of texts and materials, learning time was spent listening to what the teacher said or reading from a textbook or writing material that was written on the chalkboard. Memorization of ideas was paramount rather than the representation of ideas and the creation of images associated with those ideas. Many of the conditions necessary for real, meaningful learning of powerful ideas were therefore not present. The pedagogy did not allow students to use, or engage with, their experiences in the learning of subject matter, nor did it allow students any interaction or questioning of the ideas with their teachers. This transmission model of teaching is not effective for the majority of students, although some students of high academic ability and verbal fluency do learn in this way. It is not recommended for students with average or below average ability, those with a limited sight vocabulary, or those who have problems in reading. Further, Gurian and Stevens (2004) found that this method may place boys at a disadvantage, since girls more so than boys at this age appear to have mastered most of the auditory and other literacy skills required to learn effectively by this method.

The conditions for meaningful learning or learning for understanding are essential if we want students to master powerful ideas that can be remembered and applied in different situations and circumstances. Whether it is called learning for understanding, constructivist learning, or active learning, teachers who aim for this kind of learning strive to stimulate students' cognitive processes such as thinking, comparing, applying, deducing, concluding and creating. Perkins, in examining the many ways in which schools should help students deal with knowledge, refers to the four major skills of creating, communicating, organizing and acting on knowledge (2004, 14–15). These are the "knowledge arts" that teachers should promote if they want their students to handle knowledge well; they do so when they strive to establish a classroom culture of inquiry and excitement. Ancess (2004) and Ennis and Macauley (2002) emphasize the importance of meaning making without which learning is simply memorizing the words of others. "In classrooms that foster meaning making, teachers expect students to raise questions about the inevitable dilemmas, confusions and contradictions they uncover as they attempt to make sense of their world" (Ancess 2004, 36). These and many other educators recognize that listening and making notes are not enough, and that the skills of the knowledge arts must be made a part of teaching. These skills are especially important in a system that relies so heavily on examinations to sort students.

When teaching and learning are viewed as a transaction, a conversation or interaction between teacher and student, opportunities for the student to pose questions, to seek help in gaining understanding or clarification seem essential. For most of the teachers in this study, providing additional help or even providing the opportunity to ask for help seemed beyond their definition of their role, though they may have seen it as appropriate for class 9A. In fact, teachers who relied on students' questions to indicate their understanding or lack of it were also convinced that 9X students did not want additional help. How can this be explained when they were aware of the students' low level of performance? It seems that students' misbehaviour and disruptiveness were misinterpreted by teachers as a lack of motivation and commitment to learning.

If the process of learning is a transaction, 9X students were systematically denied one aspect of that transaction. Only two of the students interviewed were able to get additional help at home. This is understandable given the parents' level of education and their availability to provide this kind of help. The majority of those interviewed said that they relied on their friends in class – those who understood – to help them and to explain difficult concepts. Their need for additional help was evident in their stated desire to have the school provide additional help or extra tutoring. In these various ways, the pedagogy further reduced students' access to knowledge and to learning.

When we combine this pedagogy with what students saw as an uncaring relationship with most of their teachers, the conditions for optimum learning did not exist. The relationship between teacher and student is critical because it has to do with the development of trust. Such trust is critical to achieving learning and conforming behaviour. Students were willing to work for the teachers whom they loved and trusted. For these students, it appears that love and trust went together. They wanted to have loving teachers so that they could work for them.

The ways in which the pedagogy affected student learning can be seen in students' responses to and evaluations of teaching. The pedagogy did not engage students' interest and appeared to alienate some students. They did not always understand, they were bored and did not pay attention. Pedagogy influenced the depth of the curriculum and the understanding gained therefrom. Students were unable to develop a flexible understanding of subject matter that would allow them to apply that knowledge in various situations. Instead they struggled with the written word on their own or with peers, ending up with a textbook understanding of what was taught.

The inefficient use of time in the classroom was another aspect of the teaching method that had an indirect effect on learning and students' access to knowledge. In the description of the construction of disruptiveness in classroom 9X, it was shown that there were often periods of down time in the classroom during which students were not engaged in learning. Down time in the classroom was attributable not only to this primitive technology of teaching but also to frequent teacher lateness. All these occurrences had the effect of reducing the available time for teaching and learning, reducing the time students spent on tasks and the time they spent engaging with subject matter. These factors all reduced students' access to knowledge and learning.

Students' Individual Characteristics

In addition to environmental, structural and pedagogical factors, there were individual characteristics of students that influenced behaviour, learning and achievement. These characteristics included academic ability, interest in the subject, personal qualities such as ability to control one's behaviour and follow school rules, and commitment to learning. Some students – usually boys – were quick to take advantage of periods of down time to "liven up" or disrupt the class by talking, walking around, giving jokes, throwing paper planes across the room or simply beginning their own conversation, while others remained quiet or completed their work during these periods. Differences in students' academic ability were evident in students' responses to the curriculum, their ability to follow explanations in class and the grades obtained on term examinations. There were also differences in students' interest in a subject. Their interest in a subject was dependent on whether they would be taking that subject in the CXC examination (preparation for which would begin in grade 10) and whether they received good grades in that subject. All these factors influenced students' commitment to the subject and their engagement in learning tasks.

Students also varied in the level of absenteeism from school. While a few students had perfect attendance records, and many were absent only infrequently, others were frequently absent from school. Of the forty-two students in 9X, fourteen students were absent twenty or more times during the 2003–4 academic year; five were absent twenty to twenty-nine times; four were absent thirty to thirty-nine times; and five were absent more than forty times. However, although absence has been shown to be related to academic achievement, this was not the case for 9X. The rate of absence was compared with academic achievement for those students who did well and those who did poorly. The average grades of those who were absent less than forty times ranged from 55.8 (first place) to 36.9 (twenty-sixth place) in the June 2004 examination. However, those who were absent more than forty times had lower average grades with none obtaining above 45.6.

In summary, many factors contributed to the construction of academic achievement at Hillview High, and each contributed in different ways. Initial differences in achievement in grade 8 were interpreted as differences in student ability and potential which led to students being placed in different streams. These abilities, constructed during the first year and made evident in the end-of-year exam, were then accentuated by the practice and structure of streaming. In some respects, students' ability was organized through streaming. Being placed in a different stream affirmed students' academic ability and legitimated the pedagogy used. The curriculum and pedagogy provided a complex pattern of opportunities for the construction of achievement and ability. Most significant was the pedagogy used in most lessons, teachers' expectations of students, the disruptiveness caused by students' peer culture, and the learning environment that was created. Each of these influenced the others, interacting to produce learning and non-learning, participation or lack of it and ultimately student learning and achievement.

How did students reconcile their academic self-concept with their academic achievement and, when this happened, their failure to understand what was taught? They had witnessed a steady decline in their grades over the three years that they had been at Hillview High. All those who were interviewed were aware of the grades they had obtained in the December exams. Generally, students' achievements and abilities are legitimated through the grades and certificates awarded by the school, yet these grade 9 students still considered themselves to be bright and capable of succeeding at school as long as they worked hard. They still had a fairly high self-concept of their ability, and were able to separate ability from results. They felt that their actual level of achievement was influenced by the quality of teaching and, to some extent, by the disruptive culture that often existed in the classroom. The many issues that they faced at home may also have been seen as a contributing factor.

However, it was not only achievement that was constructed in the daily interactions between teachers and students and among students. These interactions and messages also had an effect on students' self-concept and self-esteem as well as their identity, personality and character. The shaping of students' academic self-concept is in the hands of teachers. On a daily basis, students in 9X observed differences in teachers' expectations compared with other streams such as 9A, and in the effort and commitment made by their peers compared with students in some other classes. They observed or experienced first hand how teachers taught, spoke and interacted with them, and they heard teachers' assessments of themselves as students. The practice of shaming, being insulted and demeaned by teachers was very common in teacher-student interactions. Some students felt that they had no power, even in the face of adult infractions and disrespect.

Nevertheless, they did not passively accept the negative evaluations of others and the treatment of those in authority. Although, more than anything else, they wanted the benefits of an education, they contested and resisted the disrespect from teachers, the physical punishment and insults and the poor teaching. Some were bold enough to contest openly and to resist, or at least to question. Most, though, opposed these actions in a covert manner, through gestures, rolling of the eyes, hissing of teeth, or angry outbursts when the teacher was absent. They developed a student peer culture which often acted as a buffer, easing their powerlessness, the harsh effects of punishments, insults and hard to understand lessons. In some respects, theirs was a subversive culture that was opposed to the dominant culture of the school and its many routines although, in the presence of authority figures, it was concealed through compliance or silence. Students, on the whole, had an uneasy, even negative, relationship with teachers.

Connell (1994) has argued that public schools and their working-class clientele inherit a deeply ambivalent relationship. He based this on a historical analysis of the experiences of poor children in schools in several countries such as Japan, Australia, the United Kingdom and the United States. On the one hand, education and schools present, for these students, the main and sometimes only promise of a better life by providing the credentials which in turn provide access to society's goods and benefits. But at the same time, public schools represent for many, especially the poor and the marginalized, repression and punishment. All schools have coercive power, as a result of the legal rights accorded to them and the reliance of other institutions in the society on their evaluations of students. So all students have to accept or tolerate schooling in all its forms as a necessity, even though they experience daily its minor irritations, its boringness and its punishments. At Hillview High, this ambivalence toward school was quite evident. Students were often excited about school, but this excitement was tempered by their disappointment with poor teaching practices and the negative treatment at the hands of adults. They liked some of their teachers and some subjects, but they also experienced first hand the institution's power, its punishment and its potential to humiliate. They chafed at the punitive and uncaring practices, and questioned many rules and procedures. But, in the end, they were willing to tolerate school and its harsh conditions because of their strong desire for an education. This contestation and this tolerance are part of the experience of high schooling in Jamaica.

These contestations and the support received from the peer culture could have blunted the effect of the negative teacher-student interactions and school practices, though these must have had an effect on some students or on all students to varying degrees. As was shown earlier, 70 per cent of these students felt good about themselves all or most of the time. But the remaining students felt this way only sometimes, rarely or never. Almost one-third of them felt that they did not belong in school or were undecided about the matter. While these sentiments are in part a result of home and community "issues", the conditions at school cannot be ignored. And while their effects on students' feelings about self appear minimal, if we consider their self-assessments provided on the questionnaire, the effects of such experiences are usually made manifest in the long term, affecting students' efficacy, self-esteem and self-confidence.

Education makes a big difference to one's chances in life and one's employability. When we compare the students in 9A with those in 9X, we see that 9X students will be at a distinct disadvantage with respect to achievement and certification. In addition, the learning environments in 9X and 9A produced different outcomes on the part of students in terms of their academic focus and attention, diligence, concentration, ability to work towards a stated goal, and to be able to follow the instructions and directions given by those in authority. All these attributes and abilities make a big difference in later employment. Students in 9A experienced more often the benefits of hard academic work, which had a positive effect on their motivation and confidence. It is in these ways that the two groups of students were prepared differently for the future and may have different life chances.

In many respects, the aspirations of 9X students were similar to those of middle-class students. When asked what career they would like to pursue in life, professions such as the following were frequently mentioned: businessperson (five students), accountant (four), engineer (four), pilot (four), lawyer (three), flight attendant (four), teacher (two), computer technician (two), doctor (two), and owning one's own business (three). A few wanted non-traditional careers such as to be a travel consultant, track star, or singer. When they were asked how they envisaged their lives in ten years' time, students saw themselves at college or university, being a successful businessperson, going abroad, or working. Many envisaged a life that they perhaps had only observed among the upper and middle classes – working, having a good job, a house and a spouse, working with some money invested, being able to drive a car to work, or just being independent. Their aspirations were normal ones that most adolescents nurture. They continued to nurture firm beliefs in themselves and their future. Their continuing attendance at school under these adverse conditions may be attributable to these aspirations. Few dropped out of school. Their parents, who themselves had a strong belief in education, also exercised a strong influence on their remaining in school. And perhaps they stayed in school because there were few alternatives open to them. Only parents who can afford it are able to provide alternative educational arrangements for their children.

What part did class play in the achievement of students in 9X? In examining the main factors that influenced achievement, some of the students' individual characteristics such as frequent absenteeism can be linked to class. The issues that they faced at home and their poverty could also be influenced by their class position. Yet most students in 9A were similarly placed. So how is class related to the level of achievement of 9X? Some have argued that, although class is a significant factor in making many social determinations, it does not usually operate as a single factor. Depending on the situation, it is considered together with other attributes such as behaviour, manners, speech and dress. However, depending on the context, behaviour and class may not be sufficient in making a determination about a person. In the case of Hillview High School, students also had to show potential and willingness to work, in addition to manners, decorum and compliance.

According to Austin-Broos (2001), education serves as a means for maintaining the social hierarchy formed in part by class differences. She argues that education, and in particular the dual system of education, has served the logic of Jamaica's class relations. At the bottom of the class scale, class can confer a kind of castelike status. One can overcome this status – this heritable identity – by virtue of education and other attributes important to the society. But getting that education is complex. In the case of students in 9X, the behaviour and disruptiveness of most of the students may have served to tie them to their class position by alienating teachers who had the power to help release them from this class position through success in education. Teachers' negative reaction to their disruptiveness influenced the quality of teaching and their commitment to these students.

Some students recognized this dynamic but they were powerless to change it, because they could not alter the peer culture that had developed. Teachers' reactions and interactions, their responses to students, and the absence of representations and networking on behalf of 9X students, together with students' poor performance on exams, all worked together to result in a winnowing of the chaff from the grain. By the time students had reached grade 10, it was clear who would make it and who would be left behind. When we compare 9A and 9X, the heritable identity of class did not lead automatically to educational failure. It was combined with other attributes, such as behaviour, manners and ability to follow rules, to have the influence that it did.

So while, officially, the dual system of education has ended and all secondary schools have now been upgraded to high school status, the social cleavages derived from the class system have been difficult to eradicate. Some students in the same school gain more from their education than others. The process through which this occurs is complex as it is structured in part by streaming and influenced by peer culture, and students' discursive and behavioural practices. It is very obvious that, in Jamaica, education is an important consideration in the determination of one's class. But not all students can "get" that education. Some students can overcome the "heritable identity" of class through education while others experience difficulty in doing so.

At the same time, the discourse on education incorporates the notion of individual achievement, a notion that is tempered with the understanding that opportunities for achievement are few and the constraints are many. This was evident at Hillview High School. For each grade level, not all students will make it to the CXC examination.[1] As Austin-Broos argues, Jamaicans' ideas about education and achievement laud individual achievement. But for working-class students to achieve with their heritable identity, they have to be aware of the institutional demands of school – displaying potential, willingness to work, proper behaviour, manners, decorum and compliance with school rules. Not all working-class students can meet this challenge. Unfortunately, most working-class students are even unaware that those are the basic requirements for success at school.

Theorizing Academic Achievement

Various explanations for students' academic achievement were discussed earlier and are presented in more detail in appendix 2. How helpful are these theories in explaining why students in 9X did and did not achieve academically at Hillview High School? The social reproduction theory, which focuses on the school's effort to reproduce the existing social and economic inequalities, will not be examined here since it does not provide specific details about what happens in schools. The cultural reproduction theory, which emphasizes the role of students' cultural capital and the ways in which the school rewards the knowledge and skills that students bring to the school, is a theory that is very plausible to educators because it addresses not only knowledge but attitudes, behaviour, manners and linguistic competence, all of which are important in any institutional setting and which influence learning. In this study, we saw the ways in which disruptiveness on the part of some students in 9X affected not only learning but teachers' attitudes to students and to teaching them. The behaviour of the students in 9A was opposite to that of 9X, and this made a great deal of difference to the way in which teachers approached the two classes. When teaching 9A, teachers made greater preparation of the lessons and sought to engage their students in learning: an approach that ultimately led to the students' academic achievement. The opposite was seen in the case of 9X. The theory of cultural reproduction has some merit in explaining academic achievement and this study showed specific ways in which it has this effect. At Hillview High School, the theory is applicable in part because of the system of streaming. However, the theory does not predict academic achievement for all students. Because streaming was such a powerful factor shaping teachers' and students' expectations, it is difficult to disentangle the effects of streaming from cultural production.

The cultural ecological theory of academic achievement considers the value placed on the social group as well as the treatment of the group by the wider society. It also speaks to students' psychological adaptation to this valuation and treatment in the form of reduced expectations and resistance to school. While this study did not examine the specifics of this theory, because of the focus on school related factors, the student interviews did not reveal disenchantment nor reduced expectations for school. Like their middle-class counterparts, these students thought that they were bright and had the ability to learn, and wanted more than anything else to be able to pass their CXC examination and continue their education.

This group of students differed by class not race. Class was made manifest in this school in a number of ways, but mainly at the level of discourse and behaviour. It was evident in the kind of "issues" that students faced and in the school culture demonstrated in the classroom. Students brought their accustomed reactions to situations and their accustomed behaviour from home to the classroom. Not only were there moments of classroom disruptiveness, but moments of sudden eruption of anger and frustration vented through shouting and physical contact. Class was also evident in some teacher-student confrontations and in exchanges with some parents. In one exchange with parents at a Parent-Teacher Association meeting, the parents were addressed in a way that they probably would not have been if they were middle-class parents at a traditional high school. Throughout the study, the quality of the discourse with students reflected a lack of respect that is typical of a demeaned group. But while teachers' demeaning discourse with students may have dampened students' motivation, hurt their feelings, reduced their interest in a subject, or caused them to not respect a teacher, parents' and students' psychological adaptation in the form of lowered expectations of education were not evident in this study. In this study there was no evidence that manifestations of class were related to the level of students' academic achievement. In Jamaica, there has been a historical reliance on education as a means of upward social mobility, and one's class or race has never deterred Jamaicans from this expectation. The psychological adaptation that is a critical part of the cultural ecological theory is not and has never been present in the Jamaican context. Thus, this theory, which was developed on the basis of the specific experiences of one racially subordinated group, has limited applicability in this school in explaining academic achievement.

The cultural production theory highlights students' production of an oppositional peer culture that works against the norms, values and goals of the school. One of the most important dimensions of school life, especially for adolescents, is the need to belong, gain popularity and not be seen as too different from peers. The disruptive and inappropriate behaviour of the students in 9X reflected what students had learned in their communities. It was not a culturally produced response to demonstrate their common identity, as this theory would suggest. Such disruptiveness reduced instructional time as well as time available to be spent on tasks, thus reducing students' access to learning. Although the behaviour of some students disrupted classrooms and teaching, these students engaged in this behaviour because they were not academically engaged or stimulated by the lesson, not because they wanted to make an ideological statement. And so, although an oppositional behaviour was manifested, this theory does not provide an adequate explanation for academic achievement because the origins of the behaviour were so different from what is posited by the theory. Nevertheless, this theory does alert educators to the possibilities of a student subculture that can work against the ethos and the goals of the school and signals the need to address aspects of the peer culture in the organization of the school.

The cultural support network theory examines the ways in which opportunities for gaining access to cultural and social benefits within the school can influence one's academic achievement. At Hillview High School, in grade 9, these opportunities came primarily in the form of recommendations for a change of stream for those students who were academically able and well behaved. For example, such connections and opportunities influenced in part the promotion to a higher stream of five students who did well in the June 2004 examination. While their performance in the examination was the important consideration, a few teachers had been advocating for some time for students, such as Andrew and O'Neill, to be moved to another stream. Apart from opportunities to change stream and teachers' recommendations in this regard, social networks that connected students to opportunities to gain social and cultural capital were rarely observed in the first year of the study. However, in the second year when the 9X students were in grade 10, I was asked by a few teachers about scholarships and other mechanisms for access to the tertiary level for deserving students. This kind of information represents the networks that can make a difference for students. The fact that examples of such networks were not prevalent in this school does not invalidate this theory. It means that, in this school, there were not many opportunities for gaining access to social and cultural knowledge that make a difference to students' academic lives.

The final theory has to do with the curriculum, specifically the extent to which culturally relevant knowledge is critical to students' learning and achievement. In this case, curriculum cannot be dissociated from pedagogy. Advocates of a curriculum grounded in culturally relevant knowledge recognize that the success of such a curriculum in enhancing students' learning is intimately connected with pedagogy. To be pedagogically effective, the teacher has to integrate the students' own knowledge and experiences into the curriculum and the teaching/learning process. In a centralized curriculum, such as that which exists in Jamaica, teachers are guided by what is prescribed in the national curriculum. Nevertheless, they can make the curriculum culturally relevant by making students' experiences and ways of thinking part of the learning framework. Such integration of students' knowledge and experiences rarely happened at Hillview High School, and the neglect of these experiences and prior knowledge was one of the striking features of the teaching observed. This was one of the aspects of the pedagogy analysed earlier and explains why students did not connect sufficiently with curricular knowledge, thus their failure to learn and achieve at a high level. This theory focuses on the curriculum, on knowledge and its cultural relevance to students' lives – an aspect that was not examined directly in this study. Nevertheless, this study has shown that the curriculum is critical to students' learning and understanding, especially as it relates to its translation into curriculum tasks and students' cognition. That critical intersection of curriculum and pedagogy is a significant consideration in students' learning and achievement. The construction of learning and academic achievement at Hillview High School was a result of the interaction of environmental, structural, pedagogical and individual factors described earlier.

Aspects of each of the five theories can be seen to be relevant in the case of this high school, but the significant explanations are specific to this high school and its special features – the socio-cultural characteristics of the students and their socio-economic status; the teachers' preparation for and commitment to teaching students with these characteristics; the capacity of the school to make compensatory provisions for students who required it and parents who were unable or unwilling to work with the school for ongoing involvement in their child's learning. In the final chapter, these aspects of schooling and the ways in which schools can be transformed into places of promise, providing education for all, will be discussed.

Note

1. In 2002, 188 out of 260 students sat the CXC English Language examination, which all candidates are required to take. But not all these students would have been allowed to take four or more subjects. The number of subjects taken depends in part on ability and performance on exams. In the 2003–4 school year, there was at least one grade 11 class from which no student was sent forward to sit the CXC examination.

Chapter 7   Improving Teaching and Schooling

Modernist views of the school emphasize its role in the cultural and social shaping of the young, and in providing knowledge and discipline that have national, regional and now global significance: "Schools interject an educational mission of extra-local proportions" (Levinson and Holland 1996, 1). In this modernist view of the school, schools build on the work of the family and have ameliorative effects on individuals and, ultimately, on the nation state and society. This view of the school does not specify the nature of the family and its relation to the school and the wider society, nor does it consider the economic and social conditions of the nation state. Nevertheless, it influences the public perception of the benefits of schooling. This conception of schooling has historically been more applicable for some social groups than for others. There is overwhelming evidence that students from poor, marginalized and some racially subordinated groups do very poorly in schools for reasons that have been explored in this study. In some countries, also, the response on the part of schools and of society to the poor performance of these students has been to place much of the blame on the parents, the students or their communities, leaving school structures largely intact (Deschenes, Cuban and Tyack 2001). This modernist view of the school embraces not only academic achievement in school subjects, but the students' overall development – their cultural awareness, and their social and emotional development. These aspects of the role and function of the school are not always considered when we assess the outcomes of the school.

Educational reform has tended to regard the improvement of the work of schools and of student learning and achievement as mainly a technical one in which outside expertise is applied to local schools. In this scenario, the curriculum is developed and methods and procedures are outlined and made available to local schools. Teachers may be provided with some initial training in these new policies, after which it is expected that the new reform will take root and the expected results will be achieved. This support is usually withdrawn at the end of the implementation process. This view of educational change is evident in the Reform of Secondary Education (ROSE) programme, which made provisions for initial staff development and materials and resources that supported the innovation. The construction of academic achievement at Hillview High School suggests that much is omitted when the solution is seen as one of simply providing the school with a curriculum and methods and procedures. This study has shown that the elements contributing to the construction of achievement have to do with the environment, structural features of the school, teachers, curriculum and students, as well as the relations that exist among them. Therefore, mapping the problem of learning and achievement has to include these features, as well as the relationships that exist between students and the adults in the school.

Given the Ministry of Education, Youth and Culture's call to teachers and schools that "every child can learn and every child must learn", what would it actually mean to teach all children in such a way that this statement is true for Jamaica? What kinds of teaching practices support learning for all students? What kind of environment supports the delivery of such high standards of teaching? What existing conditions need to be changed at Hillview High School if all children are to learn? To make the call "every child must learn" a reality and not just an empty slogan, we need to address the four factors that were found to influence learning and achievement within Hillview High School – environmental, structural, pedagogical, as well as students' individual characteristics. We must also take into account what has been learned about maintaining and supporting quality teaching in schools, and what has been established as healthy development and learning oriented environments for adolescents.

The environmental features – the physical features and students' peer culture – were found to negatively affect student learning. Unfortunately, the physical feature of the environment may be difficult to change immediately. The size of the class is a result of the over-crowding seen in upgraded high schools such as Hillview High. It is a reflection of the high demand for high school places, coupled with the low availability of school places in Jamaica, especially with the new method of admission to high schools. Class size, however, cannot be singled out, as 9A had more students in the class than 9X. Changing some features of the classroom, such as extending the windows, might alleviate the heat, though not the noise. However, it has to be accepted that noise and heat are facts of life in many poor urban upgraded schools, building standards for schools notwithstanding. A second and more significant feature of the classroom environment was the peer culture, which had an effect on teachers' and students' expectations for the class as a whole despite the efforts that individuals in 9X made. If a change is to be made in students' and teachers' expectations and on their learning, the peer culture must change. This matter will be addressed when we examine the individual characteristics of students and the ways in which the school can work to effect change in this area.

The second feature that had a direct and indirect impact on learning and achievement was streaming. Despite the widespread use of streaming in high schools, there is a great deal of evidence that challenges the widely held norm that streaming or ability grouping effectively accommodates students' differences (Oakes 1992; Slavin 1990): it fails to meet expectations for improved student learning and achievement. In fact it has been shown that it increases the inequality in achievement. Furthermore, streaming has adverse consequences on the self-concept of ability and self-esteem of those students who are placed in the low stream. At Hillview High School there was also evidence that the ability composition of a class – in part a result of streaming – can have adverse effects on the social climate and the academic expectations held by both students and teachers. Academic ability and academic achievement are, in many ways, constructed as a result of these influences and expectations. It is not that students' native ability or intelligence or initial capacities such as fluency in reading are not important. They are, but the conditions for learning created in a classroom are just as important to students' performance.

The alternative to streaming is mixed ability grouping where students are assigned to classes based on criteria other than academic ability or achievement. The research on mixed ability grouping has shown that high ability students are not necessarily disadvantaged in mixed ability groups (Slavin 1990), and there is some evidence that in some Jamaican schools where mixed ability grouping is practised, the average grades for students in mixed ability groups and high streamed groups are the same (Evans 1999). Streaming makes teaching easier for teachers but, as we have seen, it also reduces learning for the majority of students in the streams that are not classified as high ability. Having classes consisting of students of mixed ability classes will not be easy, however, as it will place greater demands on students and teachers. For students, it will mean creating a climate that will allow them to take turns teaching and learning from their peers; teachers will be required to make greater use of teaching methods appropriate for mixed ability groups. It will also require an organizational structure at the school whereby teachers can continue to learn and share ideas about teaching students grouped in this fashion.

The third feature that contributed significantly to student learning and academic achievement was the pedagogy practised in 9X. The transmission model of teaching, the absence of instructional materials and the focus on the written or spoken word resulted in a loss of interest among students and their inability to understand concepts. Teachers taught in traditional ways that appeared to take little account of student learning or the challenge of getting all students to learn. This was done in spite of the clear suggestions made in the curriculum guide about using teaching methods that reflected a student-centred and progressive approach, and in spite of reminders, prominently displayed in the teachers' staff room, of ways to increase students' expectations and improve their learning and critical-thinking skills. Teaching at this school did not, for the most part, reflect the educational reform initiatives.

The quality of teachers and teaching is critical to students' learning and academic achievement. To improve teaching and to ensure quality teaching, professional development should be provided to teachers on an ongoing basis. While there were a few teachers at Hillview High School who met the standards of good, progressive teaching, the data does not indicate that they reached this level of expertise because of special arrangements at the workplace. They had qualities that made them teach in ways that were student-centred and respectful of students. To improve teaching quality and to have teachers committed to students' academic achievement, one cannot rely on the one-shot staff development associated with reforms: research has shown it to be ineffective over time. Nor can we rely on initial teacher preparation. Critical to maintaining and developing teacher expertise are the conditions at the school that allow teachers to maintain a focus on student learning and on the challenge of making the curriculum real and meaningful for their students. These conditions enable teachers to engage in the intellectual work of curriculum and lesson planning and the advancement of subject matter knowledge (Darling-Hammond 1995; Darling-Hammond and McLaughlin 1999; Warren Little 1999). To create such conditions requires a new way of organizing teachers' work.

Teachers' work is organized around the curriculum. Any intellectual challenge that they obtain from teaching comes from their engagement with their subject matter, and the various ways in which they can communicate it to their students. Teachers have to broaden and deepen their knowledge about their subject matter as well as think about ways of teaching that subject matter. Such broadening and deepening are best done collaboratively where ideas are shared and developed in conversation with other teachers. Such engagement with subject matter informs curriculum and lesson planning. At Hillview High School, teachers for the most part worked individually. They did their lesson planning on an individual basis, although some curriculum planning and discussion took place departmentally. Teachers planned individually because their work load did not allow them to work and plan collaboratively, and also because of a tradition of teachers working individually. Because lesson planning took up so much time and most teachers had such a heavy workload, many teachers planned by outlining the content to be covered in their lessons. As one teacher explained, "Planning the lessons takes a lot. . . . It takes a lot to sit down and think about charts and how you are going to do it. [So] you just plan for the content for each lesson, you don't plan for instructional activities or materials." As professionals, therefore, teachers functioned in a bureaucratic centralized system in which the curriculum was prepared and forwarded to schools and teachers, and where the criteria for the evaluation of their work were determined by the Ministry of Education, Youth and Culture. Within the school, they were autonomous individuals who made decisions about lesson plans individually, without the benefit of ideas from their colleagues.

This organization is not the ideal one for teaching. Uniformly high levels of student achievement are not often accomplished by teachers working alone. Teachers must work together to share their ideas, experiences and knowledge about the optimal ways of teaching. Teachers must talk with each other about students, grades, learning and the many and varied ways in which the curriculum can be taught, so students can learn. They need to engage in conversation with other teachers in order to figure out the best ways in which principles of teaching and learning can be put into effect. They have to do more than present information to students verbally or in writing. Like all complex tasks, ambitious learning-centred teaching requires, "the development of strong lateral relations" (Warren Little 1999, 234). It requires the exchange and sharing of information about students, curriculum and teaching methods, as well as about student progress. We have seen in this study that when teachers work alone without strong collegial collaborative networks and support, and without an administration that monitors quality, they take short cuts that make teaching become "just talking to students".

The immediate and critical task of the teachers at Hillview High School working collaboratively will be to improve students' learning and academic achievement. The challenge will be to elicit productive intellectual work from students. How is this achieved with a centralized curriculum and a content outline sent to the school? To teach working-class students well in disadvantaged schools requires a shift toward a more negotiated curriculum (Connell 1994, 137). Teachers have to generate ideas that are relevant to the students and that connect to their lives. This process of generating ideas is best done collaboratively, and Blythe and Associates (1998) have described such a process. The breadth of available knowledge is vast. Teachers work together to generate ideas that are relevant to their students, interesting to the teachers, connected to one another and linked to major issues. It is only when there is interconnectedness among ideas that critical thinking on the part of students is possible. With such a rich array of ideas and issues, mastering a curriculum is no longer confined to having the one right answer. It is no longer memorizing the "facts" that were written on the chalkboard, because "facts" have to be contextualized and analysed. Given the amount of knowledge now available to us through a variety of means, including the internet, a rich curriculum cannot be limited to a list of topics in a curriculum guide. Nor can it be confined to any prescribed text.

This negotiated curriculum and the rich array of topics generated through joint work have to be taught to students in ways that engender understanding and that capture students' interest. Teachers working collaboratively have to give thought to the pedagogy and the challenge of teaching their students. As the principal of Hillview recognized, the teacher can no longer just talk to the students. Their needs must be taken into account and the methods and technologies to which they have become accustomed have to be employed. In addition, attention and care must be given to the cognitive skills students use in working with the subject matter – the curriculum task or task content (Doyle 1983, 1992) or to what Perkins (2004) calls the "knowledge arts" – the performances that students must engage in in order to develop and demonstrate understanding. Teachers working together can clarify the goals that they want their students to work toward (rather than simply writing notes in the notebooks) and they can, working together, generate the various activities that can achieve those goals. The pedagogy must allow students to engage in activities that allow them to do thought provoking and challenging tasks and to engage meaningfully with ideas and topics.

This new method of teaching, which focuses on student learning, will require that student learning outcomes be monitored. At Hillview High School, there was no one responsible for overseeing student learning overall or the level of achievement of any one student or class. Even though each teacher is, in principle, responsible for the learning outcomes in his or her subject, the absence of a system of accountability for students' outcomes placed the responsibility for a student's lack of learning on no one. If there had been someone or some group of teachers with responsibility for tracking student learning and achievement, that person or group would have discovered that, at the end of these students' first year at Hillview High, most students in grade 7X obtained a grade of less than 40 per cent in religious education, and sixteen students received a grade of zero. When such monitoring is done at each grade level and when there is a team responsible for student learning, corrective action can be taken as soon as it becomes necessary.

A yearly analysis of the performance of students in each subject can serve to identify weaknesses on the part of teachers and students very early and continuously in the students' career. The steady decline in 9X students' grades compared with 9A over the three years should also have been a signal that some aspect of the learning environment in 9X was detrimental to learning. This kind of monitoring should be one aspect of the "flow of information" that informs the work of a learning oriented teacher workforce. This systematic study of students' work by those who are responsible for student learning represents a stance of inquiry into teaching and learning and is an acknowledgment of a school's commitment to student learning. It signals that teachers have a shared responsibility for students' learning. A structure at the school that facilitates ongoing monitoring of students' achievement and a "flow of information" about students and their learning is necessary in a school that believes that all students can learn and all students must learn. An individual approach to organizing the workplace of teachers no longer works effectively. The new approach to organizing the work of teachers in Jamaican schools will require a great deal of effort on many fronts for teachers to change their accustomed ways of teaching. Tradition and traditional teaching practices exercise a great deal of influence on teachers, their beliefs and practices. Teachers teach in the way they were taught and the routines of teaching are difficult to dislodge (Feiman-Nemser and Remillard 1995). To change the way teaching is done requires more than a curriculum sent from the ministry to the schools, and initial workshops that inform teachers about the content and rationale of the new reform. It requires ongoing support for teachers in their effort to change their teaching practices, and it requires a structure such as the one recommended here that requires teachers to become an important part of an improvement process.

The fourth feature that had an effect on learning in 9X was the individual characteristics of students, such as level of maturity, ability to control behaviour and follow school rules, and to maintain discipline and self-control in interpersonal interactions. In most cases, students were displaying their learned behaviours acquired from home and community. Some students had difficulty adjusting to the norms of the school, while others did not wish to adjust. The personal characteristics of some students helped to create the classroom climate and the disruptiveness that so affected student learning and achievement in 9X. Coleman (1987) has argued that families at all socio-economic levels are becoming ill-equipped to provide a setting for children's optimal development – the setting that schools are designed to complement and augment in preparing the next generation. What is now missing, Coleman argues is social capital. Coleman concludes that schools will have to provide this social capital so that this becomes available to the next generation. This is especially so in the case of some working-class students. In the case of Hillview High School, and many other high schools in Jamaica, parents cannot be expected to have the academic curricular knowledge that can support their children's learning. In some cases, they may be unable to provide the norms for behaviour expected by the school, a matter that is increasingly the cause of dissatisfaction on the part of teachers.

The need to address this issue of the conflicts and contradictions between the home/community and the school is becoming more critical, as communities face more and more economic and social crises. One solution is for schools to be reoriented so that they become places where students are placed at the centre of the school (for without students, there would be no schools) and so that they provide activities that create belongingness and connectedness among students. In such schools, there is an ethic of caring which influences all interactions and relationships. Advocates of this approach argue that when schools become more of a caring community, and students feel they are a cherished part of that community, they act in ways that reflect the norms of the school. To address the problem of conflicting norms and undesirable behaviours, they recommend that schools create a caring and supportive environment rather than focus on punishing misdemeanors. Advocates such as Schaps, Battistich and Solomon state that in such a school, "students are valued contributing members of a group, dedicated to shared purposes of helping and supporting each other as they learn and grow together" (1997, 128). Such a school would also be characterized by respectful, supportive relationships among students, teachers and parents, an emphasis on common purposes and ideals, by frequent opportunities to help and collaborate with others, and by frequent opportunities for autonomy and influence. Noddings, who advocates a similar goal for the school, believes that schools should develop an ethic of care which is thoroughly relational: "It is the relation to which we point when we use the adjective caring" (2002, 14). Noddings recognizes the difficulty of creating such communities, especially when there are so many differences between teachers and students and among students, but it is absolutely critical for schools to do so in today's world, when dissent and violence are on the increase.

Proposals such as those set out by Schaps, Battistich and Solomon, and Noddings create the conditions whereby students can be involved in and contribute to the life of the school, whereby they can feel respected, and can develop the capacity to be moral agents. When schools create these conditions, they also lay the foundation for the development of students' character, since it is through activities and relationships that character, personality, and social and emotional capacities are built. Paying attention to these aspects of students' development does not minimize attention to the cognitive and the academic. Schaps, Battistich and Solomon (1997) make it clear that these conditions for building character also contribute to the conditions for creating important and engaging learning opportunities. When schools create conditions for character development, they are also creating the conditions for learning. Noddings, who advocates an alternative approach to determining curriculum, is careful to show the many ways in which these activities can be combined with the learning of ideas, as well as with other "centres of care" such as the environment, and relationships with significant others: "The crucial emphasis should be on the relevance of the subjects to self-understanding and growth" (2002, 97). These suggestions for character development are echoed by Jackson (1997) and researchers in the National Study of Adolescent Health (Bearman, Jones and Udry 1997). These solutions fly in the face of traditional approaches to dealing with deviance, require a longer term perspective on the solutions, and demand more commitment and personal caring on the part of teachers and staff. They require the commitment that we saw in Mr Lawrence, the form teacher. In his work with students in 9X, and in their responses to his show of love and caring, we get a glimpse of the rewards that building caring communities can bring.

The students who achieved at Hillview High School did so in conditions of adversity at school, at home and in their strife-torn communities. Schools must recognize this. In changing schools, such as Hillview High School, there must be a simultaneous focus on creating a learning oriented community and a caring community. With respect to creating a learning oriented community, attention has to be paid to the environmental, structural, pedagogical and individual features that impeded learning. At the same time, the school must work toward becoming a caring community where young people can experience healthy growth and development in the adolescent years. Effort must be made to address those interactions that have the potential to harm students' identity and self-esteem because they create long term consequences for students and for the nation. While students can catch up with academic learning after they have left school, it is more difficult for them to change self-concept, self-confidence and a sense of efficacy. Creating a caring community where all students and all aspects of their development matter is critical.

The solutions suggested for schools like Hillview High require a change in the defining mission of the school, as well as a transformation in the structure of teachers' work, and in the activities organized by and for students. These major changes mean a radical transformation in the ethos of the school, and the goals that it defines as important. Teachers will engage in joint work to improve curriculum, teaching and learning; students will engage in joint activities aimed at character development and learning, and both will work together for the achievement of these aims. These proposals will not be easy to implement because they suggest a radical change in school culture and teacher and student behaviour. Developing this school will not be easy but it can be done. We have seen that there were some teachers at Hillview High who wanted to pay more attention to student learning. And most students responded positively to a climate of caring and involvement.

When policy makers think about ways of improving academic achievement, they usually place emphasis on the inputs to education. There are calls for new, more qualified teachers, more resources, more money. The assumption is that when these are provided, they will solve the problems of schools. All these inputs are critical to providing the financial and physical support teachers and schools need. But just as important are the human, caring relations at the school and the structures that enable and support continued teacher learning, that provide the flow of information about student learning and achievement on which teachers need to deliberate. These structures allow teachers to learn from and with each other, and to place student learning at the centre of their agenda. These relations form the basis of teaching and learning and must be addressed if we want to improve learning environments and academic achievement. The caring relations that are part of the ethos of the school will lay the foundation for optimal student development. These changes that require collaboration, joint work, and good human relations are critical but may be the most difficult to accomplish.

Appendix 1 Research Methodology and Research Design

This study examines the process of teaching and learning and the construction of academic achievement in one upgraded high school in urban Jamaica. It documents the experiences of a class of high school students as they negotiated the demands of schooling in their effort to obtain an education. This ethnographic study focuses on the structures and processes that influence learning and ultimately academic achievement. Researchers in education and educational sociology have utilized ethnographic studies of schools and schooling to gain an understanding of these processes and the connection between outcomes and structural factors within and outside the school (Willis 1977; Ferguson 2000; Dei et al. 1997; Anyon 1995; Evans 2001). Within education, a new emphasis on the inner perspective and on the study of processes and interpretation of everyday events has resulted in a shift away from more traditional positivist research designs based on quantitative forms of data collection and analysis to a focus on culture, cultural production within institutions, and social interactions among persons. Some studies examine the production of identity and achievement which are the result of all these processes and interactions (Davidson 1996; Proweller 1998). These ethnographies examine the role that schools play in our cultural life and in the lives of students.

This study falls within the tradition of critical ethnography, which goes beyond the portrayal of what exists in an institution and the description of the meaning-perspectives of participants. Critical ethnography seeks to examine the structures of domination in institutions and society in order to expose the causes of inequality. Like researchers and educators within the critical cultural studies tradition, critical ethnographers have a commitment to examining cultural practices from the point of view of power relations: the process of struggle by those who do not have power or who are marginalized within a system. These researchers are also concerned about the ways in which such persons can be given voice and empowerment (Anderson 1989). When this kind of research is conducted in post-colonial settings, it is inevitable that this critical approach is combined with a post-colonial approach to research. One of the legacies of colonialism is the dominance of subordinate relations which continue to be expressed through the attitudes that linger from the colonial experience, and the many contradictions and complexities that present themselves in societies stratified by race, class and colour. The social and historical legacy of Jamaican schools makes a critical, post-colonial perspective very relevant to an ethnographic study of schools. Critical ethnographies in education which seek to establish the causes of inequality or power relations have been conducted on the process of dropping out of school (Dei et al. 1997), on identity formation (Proweller 1998), and on resistance and cultural production at school (Jones 1989; Solomon 1992; Willis 1977).

Why Qualitative Research?

This study also falls within the qualitative research tradition and grew out of several interests and concerns about education, academic achievement, adolescents and their development, and schooling. A primary interest was to gain a better understanding of the reasons some students do not do well in school. Thus, I wanted to go beyond the quantitative data of academic achievement to examine the practices and processes within the school, including the process of teaching and learning, as well as students' subjectivities and the meanings that students and teachers make of their experiences and institutional practices. Ultimately there was an interest in learning about the school-related factors that influence students' academic achievement and in examining the role that schools play in the lives of students. Qualitative research is especially suited to examining and understanding these aspects of institutional life.

Qualitative research emphasizes the socially constructed nature of reality, focuses on the meanings that individuals make of their experiences, and stresses the processes as opposed to the outcomes of events (Bogdan and Biklen 1998; Denzin and Lincoln 2000). It allows the researcher to give voice to the individuals – in this case, the students and teachers – and to disclose and interpret behaviour and events, in light of institutional rules and expectations and participants' meanings. Researchers who choose a qualitative approach to conduct their research may do so because they have an interest in one or more of the following: understanding behaviour from the other person's frame of reference; getting the participants' meanings, that is how they define a situation and how they construe it; studying behaviour in its natural settings, and the ways in which it is influenced by its context; examining everyday life in ordinary routine settings where people live, work or play; understanding the process of events; and interpreting every day events in order to gain their meanings. The immediate and local meanings of actions as defined from the actors' point of view are critical in this type of research (Bogdan and Biklen 1998; Denzin and Lincoln 1998; Erickson 1986).

Erickson highlights the importance of interpretation and the interpretive approach as a criterion for qualitative research. The researcher is concerned with the subjective meanings as well as with "the relation between meaning-perspectives of actors and the ecological circumstances of action" (1986, 127). Furthermore, there is an assumption that the informal and formal systems in an institution operate simultaneously, that "persons in everyday life take action together in terms of both official and unofficial definitions of status and role" (128). Thus, the focus on the social ecology of the school – its process and structure – is important in research on teaching and life in schools.

Research Design

The study uses a case study approach. It focuses on one institution, examining all aspects of that institution that have bearing on the research questions, and choosing the most appropriate data gathering methods to obtain the information desired. In this case, the object of study was an upgraded high school in urban Jamaica with a focus on one grade 9 class.

The initial concerns and interests were outlined in the introductory chapter. The research questions that guided the study were: How are the outcomes of schooling, particularly students' educational achievement, related to the rituals and school practises, pedagogical practises and other aspects of schooling? What are the characteristics of learning, teaching, knowledge and knowledge acquisition that result in academic outcomes? What are the salient features of the students' life world that have an impact on the thinking and action of teachers and students? And how can the differences in academic outcomes by school or social group be explained? The main methods of data gathering used in this study were participant observation, interviewing, examination of site documents and a student questionnaire. A description of the fieldwork and the decisions made about these data gathering techniques are presented below under Research Process: Methods and Practices.

Sampling

The participants who provided data for this study were the students in grade 9X at Hillview High School, all teachers and specialist teachers of that class, the principal, vice-principal and guidance counsellors. At the start of the school year, there were forty-two students in 9X: twenty-five boys and seventeen girls. This made the composition of the class unusual in that there are usually more girls than boys at the high school level. All these students were the subject of observation. The choice of a grade 9 class for this study was a deliberate one in that these students were not yet immersed in preparing for the CXC curriculum which begins in grade 10; also because students were at the age of middle adolescence, a time when they were beginning to face many developmental issues. The choice of the particular class was made by the grade-level supervisor, after I asked that I be assigned an average class, and one whose members would not be reluctant to talk with me. I later learned that this class had a reputation for talkativeness in class, which may have been the main reason for the grade supervisor's choice.

There were six academic subjects and five practical subjects offered at grade 9. Family life education and library were also offered. All six academic subjects were observed (English language, English literature, mathematics, social studies, religious education and Spanish) as well as two of the practical subjects (principles of accounts and information technology) and two sessions of family life education. A total of twenty-four lessons was observed, including a lesson taught to grade 9A students, considered the brightest. The decision was made early in the research to sample as many subjects as possible. However, the choice and number of subjects sampled was dependent on the timetable. The following are the subjects and number of lessons observed in this study:

English Language	2
English Literature	5
Principles of Accounts	2
Social Studies	5
Religious Education	2
Science	2
Mathematics	2
Spanish	3
Information Technology	1

Two sessions of family life education were also observed. Form time, a one session period timetabled once per week and led by the form teacher, was observed eight times during the first term and four times during the second term. Other sites for observation included: Culture Day and Boys' Day at Hillview High School, a parent-teacher meeting, and a staff meeting. My involvement in these latter activities was merely as an observer. I also observed some extra-curricular activities, especially scheduled activities such as sports, activities engaged in during lunch break, in the corridors, and other places where students gathered. Six of the twelve subject teachers were interviewed. These six were chosen because they were the teachers most frequently observed. They were also interviewed when specific information was needed, such as the reading teacher, who was able to provide information on students' reading abilities and activities.

Gaining Entry

Gaining entry or access is a social process that continues even after the researcher has gained permission to conduct the study or made the first visit to the research site. It requires ongoing negotiation between the researcher and the participants, even up until the point where the study is being concluded. The politics of access – being careful about presentation of self, about who is approached and about following protocol – is present from the very first contact with a representative of the site until the stage where the researcher admits that the research has ended. It is played out in many ways during the project as relationships develop, change and evolve.

Site selection usually entails considerations such as the characteristics of the site that are of interest to the study, the size and composition of the student body, as well as a number of practical considerations, such as convenience of location. I chose a co-educational high school that attracted students mainly from low socio-economic, working-class backgrounds. The examination results on the national examinations (CXC) made this school a good candidate for a study of educational achievement. In 2002, although students at Hillview High School obtained very good passing grades in subjects such as office procedures and principles of business, they did not do as well in subjects such as English language and mathematics, which are considered critical for access to later studies and to employment. Passes in subjects such as chemistry were poor. The location of the school was also convenient as it was close to my home and work.

To make initial contact with the school, I telephoned the principal, Mr Stewart (all names in this report are pseudonyms), during the second term of the academic year prior to the study (2002–3). I informed him of my interest in doing the study and the purposes and concerns that led to this interest. I was not personally known to the principal but he recognized my name. When I asked permission to conduct the study, he readily agreed, stating that such a study was well needed and would inform the work of the school. The purpose of the study, as I explained to him, was to understand how students make sense of their school experience, and the reasons why they achieve academically at school. I placed the study in the context of being adolescents in Jamaica today when there are so many attractions and distractions for them.

My second contact with Mr Stewart was made at the end of August 2003, before the start of the first term in the academic year 2003–4. At that time, I met Mr Stewart in his office where we spoke at length about the study, the demands that would be made on the staff and students and what we hoped would be the benefits of the study. I had prepared a formal proposal of the study which he said would be discussed with the staff and with the chairman of the school board. The proposal was approved by the chairman of the school board without any problem. On the occasion of the first visit to the school, I also met Mr Murray, the grade supervisor to whom I explained the purpose of the study for the first time.

The second visit to the school took place during the first week of October. My intention on that occasion was to meet or get more acquainted with the gatekeepers, such as the grade-level supervisor and the form teacher. On that occasion, I met with the vice-principal whom I knew. I also spoke again with Mr Murray who insisted that I meet the form teacher of grade 9X. Mr Lawrence, the form teacher, was on the playing field since this was a physical education period. Mr Murray explained the research to him as a "study of behaviour patterns of the students of 9X". I later elaborated on the purpose of the study to Mr Lawrence and explained that I would spend a year with the students. I briefly explained that this is the type of research that required much time in the field and much interaction with and observation of the students.

Mr Lawrence was very warm and welcoming. I once again explained the purpose of the study elaborating on what Mr Murray had said. He expressed interest in the study and its outcomes and immediately began to acquaint me with the students who were on the playing field. We were at that point near the netball court, so he provided a brief commentary on the girls in grade 9X. We then moved on to the football playing field where the boys were preparing for a game. Here, I also received a briefing on some of the boys present. I was told of the twins, the boys who were a concern to Mr Lawrence, the boy who wanted more responsibility but who needed to show more maturity, and the three boys who came from "good homes with a mother and father", who worked very hard, and who did not give problems. On this occasion, Mr Lawrence demonstrated a knowledge of and caring for each of his students that would be demonstrated throughout the study. As he interacted with the students, I saw a relationship that I would later describe as respectful and caring. Gaining access to the form teacher therefore presented no problems.

After the physical education period, I had the chance to meet the students of 9X. Mr Lawrence and I made our way to the classroom and waited for the students to return. When they returned to the class, Mr Lawrence spoke to them about a form matter and then introduced me. I explained that the purpose of the study would be to understand what school teaching and learning were like for them. I briefly described this type of research and the requirement of my being there every week, and asked for their permission to sit in on their classes. I also informed them that later during the year I would like to speak with some of them outside of class. At the end, I asked for questions. One girl, whose name I later learned was Molly, asked if I was a psychologist. I explained my role at the University of the West Indies which included having a knowledge of psychology but stated that I was not a psychologist. Most of the students seemed interested in what was said, although some were inattentive and talking among themselves. At the end of this question and answer exchange, the students clapped. After Mr Lawrence left, I remained to observe the lesson that followed.

Gaining initial entry to the students, the form teacher and the grade supervisor did not pose a problem. However, entry or continued acceptance in the field has to be constantly negotiated. This I did by always being respectful and friendly, and always observing formalities. I tried to bridge the gap between the students and myself – a gap obvious in terms of age and status – by hanging out with the students during lunch time, attending as many form time sessions as I could, trying to make friendly conversation with as many students as would let me, and expressing an interest in what individuals were doing. For example, during a discussion at lunch, I learned that one boy was saving his money to go to a hamburger restaurant. On my next visit, I asked him if he had been able to go to the hamburger place and how much he had enjoyed it.

It was also very easy to maintain acceptance with Mr Lawrence. I tried to be at most of the form time sessions where matters relating to the development of the students or to discipline and social events were discussed. After those sessions, I was able to tag along beside Mr Lawrence, discussing some of the matters that had been raised in class or raising new issues or simply expressing interest in the students. Because of the interest he took in his students, we always had something to discuss. I took advantage of these opportunities to discuss some of my emerging themes and assertions with him, to try out ideas or verify matters that I was unsure about. Mr Lawrence became a key informant mainly because of his knowledge of the students and his willingness to talk extensively about them. As Bogdan and Biklen (1998) point out, although key informants provide very useful information to a qualitative study, there are dangers associated with relying on key informants. This matter will be addressed when I discuss issues of reliability and validity.

Gaining entry to the teachers was straightforward in most cases. Teachers were informed about the study by the principal at a staff meeting. Thereafter, I approached each of the teachers whose classes I observed when he or she arrived at the classroom to teach. I normally waited for them at the entrance to the class, and on their arrival introduced myself, referred to the study, and asked for their permission to observe. No one denied me permission, though some were more enthusiastic than others. One teacher asked me to go into further details about the study. Another seemed very uncomfortable with my being present in the class whereupon I offered to leave and return at the end of the class. He agreed. I also had to gain entry with each of the teachers whom I interviewed. This was fairly easy since interviewing was conducted during the third term, after I had observed them for two terms. By then, we knew each other fairly well and they were aware of the study. In the case of one teacher, I had to explain the purpose of the study all over again, outlining the benefits of the study to the school, before he agreed to be interviewed. I explained to all teachers that their assent to be interviewed was a special favour which did not have to be granted. It was not difficult to maintain acceptance with the grade supervisor since I not only observed his class, but tried whenever I saw him to be respectful, friendly and interested in the students. He was also friendly and continued to express interest in the study and its progress.

The Research Process: Methods and Practices

Data collection began in early October 2003 after my second visit to the school. I was in the field for the entire academic year which ended in June, 2004. I later returned to the site in September of 2004 in order to obtain additional demographic data, to administer a student questionnaire and to find out how the students had fared in their end-of-year examinations. Information on students' grades and absenteeism was obtained at this time. I also had to meet my obligation of discussing the study with the staff and the students separately. In addition, I conducted an interview with some of the eighteen students who were originally interviewed in the academic year 2003–4. I remained in the field until April 2005, although I have continued my relationship with the school in other capacities.

Participant Observation

Observation can be charted on a continuum of complete observation with no interaction to total involvement of the researcher in the setting being studied. My observation of teaching could be described as observer-participant for the most part although there were a few instances where it could be called participant-observer. The difference lay in the extent of interaction or involvement with the students and the teacher.

During the first term of the study, I visited the school roughly two times each week. The first visit lasted about half day and on each occasion, I observed about three lessons, depending on the timetable and whether the lessons were double or single sessions. The second weekly visit was made in order to do a follow up observation of a topic, or to be present at a form time session. On many second visits, however, I was able to observe other subject areas. During the first term, most of the research time was spent being an observer and, in a few cases, a participant-observer of lessons such as mathematics or English, attending form time sessions, and hanging out with the students during their lunch hour. I also sat in the classroom with the students during lunch time, in order to get to know the students and to establish rapport. Since the school had no cafeteria, students ate their lunches in the classroom. These informal gatherings of students over lunch provided an occasion to observe them in a relaxed and often friendly and jovial mood. Some of the students did not have lunch (some did not have money for lunch), so they played dominoes or read, or joked around with friends.

So in addition to observing teaching, the first three months were spent in building the trust and confidence of the students, building a relationship with the teachers whom I was observing, and developing a relationship with the administrators. In qualitative research, much of data collection depends on cultivating authentic respectful and engaged relationships with those in the field. Developing these relationships is especially important during the first months of a study but is essential throughout. During the first term of observation, I began to discern the various peer and friendship groups. Thus, the peer group became a focus of interest during the second and third terms. The pattern of visiting the school twice per week continued during the second term, when I began to interview students. These interviews sometimes replaced the form time sessions. During the third term of the first year, I continued observation and, in addition, interviewed teachers and guidance counsellors. (See appendix 3 for the interview schedule for teachers, Appendix 6 for the interview schedule for guidance counsellors.)

The focus of observation, initially, was the classroom and the interactions that occurred therein. Initially, the classroom was the obvious site for observation as this was the space where all students met as a group for instruction. The classroom provided rich data for examining the curriculum, teaching and learning, as well as students' responses to the curriculum and to teaching. The classroom was also the location where boys and girls interacted outside of teaching hours, when teachers were not present. It was also the location where form time was held, where there was an emphasis on students' personal behaviour, and where matters related to discipline were discussed. Being in the classroom provided an opportunity to observe students informally, when they were in relaxed moods, playing dominoes, reading quietly, having conversations with peers, making merry or having an angry outburst.

The study's interest in academic achievement also made the classroom an important area for observation.

Interviewing

A sample of eighteen students – ten boys and eight girls – was chosen from the forty-two students for focus group, in-depth interviewing. Each interview group consisted of three or four students, and lasted for about one hour. Boys were interviewed separately from girls in part because there were questions related to gender relations and because the intent was to interview them according to friendship groups which, in all cases, were same sex. Students were chosen on the basis of their academic focus (high and low), their apparent willingness to talk based on their behaviour in class and on friendship groups. A few students who did not fit the criteria of academic focus but who were seen as key informants on a variety of matters were also included in the sample to be interviewed. Three of the groups were interviewed on more than one occasion. The interviews were conducted in the audio-visual room which ensured some degree of privacy, and on two occasions, in one corner of the library. The interviews aimed at gaining students' perspectives on their school, teachers and teaching, their curricular subjects, aspects of their life world, and their aspirations for the future. They were conducted during the second term, after I had spent a term observing the students, although brief conversations were sometimes held with students after an observation of a class in order to clarify some aspects of what had been observed. A copy of the student interview schedule is provided in appendix 4. A questionnaire was administered to all students during the third term of the first year of the study. This questionnaire, provided in appendix 7, sought information related to students' home life, their academic self-concept, their academic achievement and their aspirations for the future.

Six of the twelve subject teachers were interviewed on matters related to their teaching, their specialist subject, their views of teaching as a career, and their views of the 9X class. A copy of the interview schedule is provided in appendix 3. Interviews with teachers lasted approximately forty-five minutes and were conducted privately at various locations at the school. The two guidance counsellors were interviewed together and separately on matters related to the students, students concerns and welfare. The reading teacher was also interviewed to gain an understanding of the problems that some students were experiencing with respect to reading. The vice-principal was interviewed once on matters related to administration, and faculty and student development. (See appendix 5 for the interview schedule for the vice-principal.) I also spoke with the principal on many occasions, although no formal interview was conducted with him. These conversations covered such topics as teaching methods used by teachers, teaching quality, teacher morale and the school's Culture Day.

Ensuring Validity and Guarding Against Bias

The importance of interpretation and the interpretive approach as a criterion for qualitative research has been highlighted by many (Erickson 1986; Bogdan and Biklen 1998; Stake 2000). In the process of gathering and making meaning of data, the researcher has to pay attention to the meanings that individuals make of events and actions. But in addition, the researcher has to pay attention to the ways in which the individual's perspectives are shaped by the context in which he or she is situated (Erickson 1986). In making interpretations, the researcher therefore has to rely on what is observed, an assessment of the meaning of the action in light of the context as well as the person's actions and interpretations of what is observed. Although the researcher is the main instrument of data collection and analysis, she has to rely on others to verify conclusions drawn. As a researcher, I used various methods to ensure validity in the data and in the conclusions that I drew. First, I avoided observer effects (whereby the participants would act differently in my presence) by spending a sufficient amount of time – more than one academic year – in the field.

Data collection lasted for more than one year. I worked hard at establishing a good rapport and a trusting relationship with the students and staff of Hillview High. I think it was clear, as the research progressed, that I was interested in them as students and as persons. I tried at all times to ensure that my actions were neutral. I never called attention to their behaviour, never asked them to be quiet even when the noise in the classroom was excessive, for that would have immediately transformed me into a teacher. I simply observed. Because of my interest in their welfare and their lives at school and out of school, and my continuing presence in their classroom, I think I succeeded in establishing this rapport and relationship with students. From their behaviour in my presence, I think they came to accept me as an interested observer in their classroom. There were several instances, for example, where students confided in me on matters related to school life or they came to ask questions on a variety of matters or showed interest in my own work.

With respect to what was observed, I obtained independent corroboration in those cases where this was necessary. This meant checking interpretations with the teacher(s), the form teacher, the administration or with other students. Questions of clarification were posed to students and staff immediately after a class or after special events. A range of subjects was sampled for observation, and lessons were observed at different times of the day, week and year in order to get a broad perspective on the teaching of that subject. Visits to the site were never pre-arranged although, after a while, I had established a pattern of visiting each week. A representative sample of students and teachers were interviewed in order to get their perspectives on evolving themes in the study and to get verification or modification or elaboration on the validity of these interpretations.

Because themes that emerged through data analysis represent a construction, it was necessary to get some verification from the participants. This was done in the extended interviews with the students and the teachers. The content of the interview was determined by these themes which were grounded in the observational data collected. During these interviews, I sought to get the perspectives on a range of issues of interest to the study but I also aimed at verification. I also verified these themes with members of the administration – especially the vice-principal, and with the form teacher. As stated earlier, the form teacher became a key informant. He had an in-depth knowledge of the students and the challenges they each faced. So he not only provided this information, but was also able to share his perspectives on some of the themes. As a teacher, Mr Lawrence has his own interpretations of and responses to student behaviour. To guard against bias or his views having undue influence on the interpretation, I treated his interpretation as another source of data which had to be combined with other sources. In addition to these sources of corroboration, I also communicated aspects of the study to the teachers during the second year of the study. Their questions and responses alerted me to some aspects of the report that needed more clarification or emphasis. For example, when a teacher suggested that if I had observed grade 9A, I would have seen a different kind of teaching, it alerted me to the importance of the effect of class culture and behaviour on teachers' perceptions and teacher-student interaction.

Ethics and Confidentiality

In any type of research, there are ethical considerations that have to do with the conditions under which the research is conducted. Two such issues relate to having informed consent, and the avoidance of risk or danger to the persons involved in the study. In qualitative research, because of the length of time spent in the field, there are additional considerations relating to the nature of the relationship that is established, the appropriateness of the methods used, the roles assumed by the researcher, confidentiality, and respect.

In this study, access was gained through the official channels, including the Ministry of Education, the school board, and the administration of the school. The research was described in as much detail as was feasible and the nature of each person's involvement was communicated before seeking his or her consent to being involved. In the case of the students, their consent was sought and given as a group. The permission of the administration and the form teacher was sought whenever I went outside of the original plan of the research, as happens in qualitative research. Teachers and students were informed of the relevant aspects of the study and teachers had the choice of being involved or not. In the case of the students, I relied on the administration's judgement that a written consent from parents was not necessary. However, all questionnaires and interview schedules to be used with the students were approved by the vice-principal. Efforts were made at all times and throughout the study to maintain confidentiality, and all participants were informed that confidentiality would be strictly adhered to. For example, in discussing aspects of the findings, the names of individual students were never discussed with teachers or administrators. In written reports, names were avoided or pseudonyms were used.

In fieldwork relationships, I tried at all times to be respectful to both students and teachers, not only because this is essential for good human relations and for obtaining valid trustworthy data, but because I was aware of the asymmetrical nature of the relationship, especially between myself and the students.

Data Management

The technical requirements of data management can be daunting, especially given the length of the study and the number of data sources. First, the observational data had to be transcribed. It is usually recommended that this be done immediately or as soon after observation as possible. Short hand notes were always taken during observation. These provided the prompts for the later elaboration and transcription of the field notes, which were usually prepared the same day or the following day. Observer comments, which represented my reflections, reactions to or questions on what was observed were noted wherever they occurred to me. These ideas occurred during the observation itself, on my way from the school, later during the day, or while I was reconstructing the field notes. Observation and the transcription of the field notes were the focus of the research process during the first term.

During this time, I began to familiarize myself with the data, reading and re-reading the narrative, notes and observer comments. Some themes and analytical questions began to emerge at this time. Because I was taking a critical perspective on the research, questions of class and gender inequality were lenses through which the observational and interview data were analysed. But my interest in academic achievement and student development made the questions of student understanding of teaching and learning salient. The analytical memos and researcher questions led to the development of initial codes. This represented the first stage of data analysis, where themes, observer comments and other initial perspectives on the data were identified.

This process also provided some basis for the interviews with the students and the teachers.

The interviews conducted during the first, second and third terms were all recorded and later transcribed and entered in Microsoft Word. Readings and re-readings of these interview transcripts yielded additional themes and codes. The interview transcripts and the field notes, as well as other data such as site documents from the field, were all combined into the entire corpus of data. A complete re-reading of all these data and a re-examination of the themes and codes represented the second stage of data analysis. The conventional method of data analysis was used by "cutting and pasting" the various coded data. These codes constituted the main sources for the assertions which, together with the evidence from the field notes and the interview transcripts, became the basis for the final report.

Appendix 2   Theories of Academic Achievement

These theories are presented in the chronological order in which they were developed. As such, they also reflect different and changing views of the importance of aspects of the environment that have an impact on the student and on learning. The first explanation, social reproduction theory, focuses on the state or society and its need for certain kinds of labour in a capitalist economy. Assuming a capitalist social system, this theory argues that, in a capitalist society, the existing social and economic system of relations must be reproduced. This is done by the various institutions of the state such as the school. To carry out this "reproductive function", the school provides education for students according to their social and economic background. By doing this, schools help to allocate students to different positions in the economic system, not according to individual merit but according to their social class or race (Apple 1972, 1996; Bowles and Gintis 1976; Karabel and Halsey 1977). When different types of schools differ in the extent to which they enable (or prepare) students to gain the valued outcomes of schooling, then this reproduction is carried out according to type of school and school allocation (Apple 1972, 1996; McLaren 1989; Connell 1985).

The social reproduction theory, also referred to as the correspondence theory, represented at the time a radical liberal critique of social inequality and the school's role in sorting students for the job market. However, it does not explain how this sorting is done, and the specific ways in which the school contributes to social inequality. This explanation has been criticized for its mechanistic view of schooling. Schools and teachers are portrayed merely as agents of the state and passive players of the roles assigned to them. The theory also fails to acknowledge human action and agency, and ignores some of the important processes of schools, such as teaching, learning, curriculum enactment and student-teacher interaction. It also does not account for the fact that some students from the subordinated groups do well at school.

Another perspective on educational achievement – cultural reproduction – inserts culture and cultural knowledge into the argument of the reproduction theorists. This explanation states that the dominant classes in society possess a distinctive cultural knowledge and set of behaviours (cultural capital) that are valued by society and by extension the schools. This cultural capital is inherited by children of the dominant classes (Bourdieu 1977; Bourdieu and Passeron 1977). This theory is based on Bourdieu's analysis of the way the French educational system functioned. Children from these families "inherit substantially different cultural knowledge and skills, manners, norms, dress, style of interaction, and linguistic facility than do sons and daughters of the lower class" (Mehan 1992, 4). Within the school, students from the dominant classes are easily able to achieve success by virtue of this cultural capital – their linguistic competence, behaviour and cultural knowledge.

This theory is more plausible to educators than the social reproduction theory since it takes into account factors that are important in the teaching/learning process and in teacher-student interaction within the school. Research has consistently shown that students' socio-economic status is positively related to their academic achievement. And common sense tells us that children of, say, professional families will learn a great deal from their parents, through the daily interactions and conversations over dinner and from parents' ability to help with homework. Nevertheless, the theory is also deterministic, and fails to explain why not all students from the dominant classes do well at school and not all students from the poorer classes fail to achieve academically. It also ignores or plays down the agency of individual teachers and students, as well as the pedagogical and curricular aspects of the school.

A third explanation for the variation in educational achievement takes into account the historical and social relations of the group to the larger society and the existence of dominant power relations of the larger dominant group in the society. This cultural ecological theory was formulated by John Ogbu (1974, 1999) with specific reference to African Americans to explain their low achievement in relation to other Americans. The cultural ecological theory of achievement "posits that there are two sets of factors influencing school performance of racially subordinated groups: how society at large and the school treat students from these groups (the system) and how racially subordinated groups respond to those treatments and to schooling (community forces)" (Ogbu 1999, 156). The system forces refer to the historical relationship of dominance, oppression, power and discrimination that are present in the wider society and replicated in the school system. The community forces that result from these system forces are expressed as a psychological adaptation on the part of African American students and their parents who develop a pessimistic view of schooling and its benefits. The students also develop a set of adaptive behaviours which include resistance to the treatment they receive at school. They become pessimistic about the value of schooling or the possibilities of achievement in a white dominated school system.

The system forces therefore create psychological adaptive responses (community forces) on the part of students and their parents. Students see that family members with an education are unable to get ahead or even get started in the job market. They experience the inequities of life at school and in the wider society. Making a cost-benefit analysis, they decide to place their energies in other directions. They therefore reduce their expectations for education and consequently the efforts they make to get an education. The cultural ecological theory places students' performance in historical and social perspective and highlights the impact of status and power relations between social groups on the achievement of the subordinate group.

Cummins, in examining the relevance of this theory to the high failure rate of subordinated groups in Canada, including students of Caribbean descent, elaborates on the cultural ecological theory by attributing students' disengagement to the loss of identity in a society where their cultural background is not emphasized or even valued. Cummins argues that the "destruction of identity, brought about by remaining trapped in oppressive school and social situations and the devaluation of [their] cultural identity and languages both in the school and in the wider society" (1997, 416) are reasons students of these subordinated groups do not do well at school. Thus, the status of the group in the wider society must be taken into consideration in understanding why students who are members of that group do not succeed. The psychological processes that link the wider social status of the group to student performance include insecurity in regard to cultural identity, and the feeling of being subordinated and devalued. Cummins and Ogbu believe that coercive power relations that exist in the wider society are translated into relations within the school – between teachers and students and among students. In order to disrupt this relationship between what exists in the wider society and what occurs in schools, Cummins recommends that teachers self-consciously become mindful of the effect of the power relations of the wider society and begin to engage in more collaborative power relations with students so that spaces can be created for students to negotiate their identity as persons with their own socio-cultural background and with their own personal qualities.

The fourth explanation for group differences in educational achievement – cultural production – highlights students' production of an oppositional culture within the school. In this case, students come to regard opposition and resistance to what they see as oppression and discrimination as essential to their identity and membership in a student subculture. Their oppositional behaviours are a resistance to the institutional structures and processes of the school, and represent their response to the low regard in which they are held by the institution, and the poor treatment they receive from members of that institution. These oppositional student behaviours influence academic achievement because there is usually a conflict between the organizational discourse of the school and the discursive and performative practices of students which are seen as a challenge to the school itself. Those who hold this theory highlight the importance of students' identity, the performative acts that reflect this identity within student subcultures, and the ways in which adults in a school interpret such behaviour and deploy it as evidence of students' poorly developed identities as learners. While students may see such behaviours as reflective of their identity and membership in a student subculture, teachers may interpret such behaviours differently, regarding them as evidence of students' lack of interest in learning, in adhering to sanctioned rules of behaviour and hence to their unteachability.

Explanations that highlight student discursive or performative practices and conflicts with school authority are based on actual ethnographic studies carried out in schools (Solomon 1992; Youdell 2003). Youdell (2003) shows how teachers' construction of "appropriate student behaviour" is often based on expectations that are class based. What is appropriate student behaviour is often at odds with what some students consider important for their subcultural identity. Their discursive/performative class-specific behaviours may include a distinct style of dress, speech or walk. These become a site for contestation and may be seen as a challenge to the adults of the school. When students do not conform to or meet adults' standards, they are marginalized by teachers who fail to develop a commitment to their learning and academic achievement. The role of students' performative practices that become part of their identity or subjectivity is relevant to countries such as Jamaica, as popular culture becomes significant in the lives of students, and as the question of student identities and subjectivities become more urgent.

The third and fourth explanations – the cultural ecological theory and the cultural production theory – speak to the ways in which power relations and oppression in the wider society influence the relationship between students from racially subordinated and low socio-economic groups and the adult authority of the school. There is a significant body of research that describes the way that students from racially subordinated and poor socio-economic groups are regarded and treated within the school. Studies from many countries including the United States, Canada, the United Kingdom, Australia and Japan all support the view that when students are treated with stigma or with lack of respect they fail to learn. In most of these case studies, skin colour or race is the signifier. But in many cases it is social class, language or being different in some way. This stigmatization occurs when the teacher is a representative of the dominant group. In cases such as these, it is not simply the action of the teacher or the action of the students but the relationship that is established or not established and the regard in which the student is held that leads to learning or not-learning on the part of the student. Erickson seems to emphasize the actions or sentiments of the student in this non-learning, although he does not ignore the role of the teacher and the school in creating the conditions for trust.

> Learning what is deliberately taught can be seen as a form of political assent. Not learning can be seen as a form of political resistance. Assent to the exercise of authority involves trust that its exercise will be benign. This involves . . . trust in the legitimacy of the authority and in the good intentions of those exercising it. (1987, 344)

Some researchers with this social/historical perspective see the problem differently, and highlight the structures and processes and, in particular, the teachers and pedagogy. In their historical analysis of how schools have treated low-status students such as immigrants and minorities, Deschenes, Cuban and Tyack (2001) state that in the United States, as in many other countries, there has historically been a mismatch between the structures of school and students from poor socio-economic backgrounds. This mismatch has led to failure on the part of these students, a failure which is constructed through segregation, labelling, and an assumption of what at one time was termed cultural deprivation or cultural deficit. The labels that have been attributed to some students who are "different" – often the poor, the foreigner and those who speak a different language and who are socially and culturally different – have included terms such as: slow, lacking in motivation, culturally different, wayward and unteachable. Such labels placed the blame for failure on the students and parents and prevented the school from examining its own structures. In other words, the problem of failure was framed as an individual student's responsibility rather than one that required changes in school structures and pedagogical approaches. This mismatch refers to the rigid application of traditional practices without taking into account special characteristics of the student body. The mismatch is a result of social inequality and the powerlessness of subordinate groups in charting or influencing the kind of education that they receive in the public schools. The structures to which Dechennes et al. refer include the rituals and practices of the school, the expectations held for students, communication patterns of teachers, administrators, and students, and the interpersonal relations between teachers and students.

A fifth explanation – the social support network theory – for the lower academic achievement of working-class and racially subordinated groups builds on the notion of cultural capital and the advantages that this brings to students. It also assumes that there are discrepancies in power relations between groups in society. But rather than focusing on the possession of this capital and the ways in which it facilitates learning, this explanation examines how possibilities and opportunities for gaining access to cultural and social capital are unevenly distributed in society and in institutions such as schools. There is an "unequal distribution of opportunities for forming relationships with agents who exert various degrees of control over institutional resources" (Stanton-Salazar 1997, 4), and this inequality is based on social status. Persons whom he describes as being "of low status" – such as working-class groups, some racially subordinated groups and, in some situations, women – do not have access to the social ties, networks and relationships with institutional agents which provide the benefits of access, cultural knowledge, mentoring and the like. Stanton-Salazar refers to this social network, ties and relationships as social capital, which generates valued resources for individuals. Middle-class people and members of in-groups use this social network on a regular basis for gaining access to society's social benefits. Low-status persons, in contrast, do not usually have these connections – this social capital – nor the knowledge and skills to gain access to it. So this theory places emphasis on the relationships of respect and trust which form the basis for students and teachers working together as they construct achievement. This relationship of trust and respect is taken for granted by mainstream middle-class groups.

When we examine the school and its developmental and educational mandate, it is clear that all students need some sort of institutional support that enables them to become fully integrated within the school system, and to be effective participants in that system. The social capital that is the focus of this theory takes the form of social relationships with institutional agents who can provide this kind of institutional support. In other words, the institutional support is based on (and is impossible without) good social relationships with persons within the institution. And it is the development of these social relationships with school agents, such as teachers, that working-class and racially subordinated students find problematic.

Stanton-Salazar (1997) outlines six key forms of institutional support which he considers key ingredients for social integration and success within the school system. These are: (a) providing various funds of knowledge that can help the student navigate the workings of the school and the educational system; (b) bridging or acting as a mediator between students and various gatekeepers, social networks and opportunities; (c) providing advocacy and making other forms of personalized intervention; (d) acting as a role model; (e) providing emotional and moral support and; (f) providing feedback, advice and guidance to students. Stanton-Salazar also emphasizes the importance of funds of knowledge and socialization into various institutionally sanctioned discourses that regulate interaction and communication and behaviours. The development of these discourses is particularly important for working-class students, in order for them to build the relationships and gain access to resources that will make a difference to their educational futures.

It is Stanton-Salazar's argument that these forms of institutional support are often taken for granted and accessed by middle-class families but are often denied low-status students. Part of the problem that working-class students and students from some racially subordinated groups face is the "construction of interpersonal trust, solidarity, and shared meaning in the context of institutional relations, which are defined, on the one hand, by hierarchical relations of power and institutional barriers, and on the other, by institutional dependency" (Stanton-Salazar 1997, 17). In other words, it is often difficult for persons to combine the existence of a hierarchical relationship and the dependency of one group on another with the development of trust, solidarity and respect. Given that students from working-class and racially subordinated groups are more dependent on agents of the school for institutional support than middle-class students, dependency (and low status) has to be combined with the development of trust and solidarity – which appears socially difficult. In addition, while institutional resources and support are transmitted on the basis of subjective biases as well as on more objective (and supposedly fair), criteria, there is evidence that there are, within the school, institutional structures that make the school experience alienating and exclusionary for these students. Stanton-Salazar refers to aspects of the school such as the superficial and transitory relations with teachers, lack of opportunities for general social exchange between teachers and students which make these relationships hard to establish. The difficulty of establishing these trusting relations between students from working-class and racially subordinated groups and school agents, such as teachers, represents the root cause for these students' physical and psychic disengagement from school.

Social antagonisms and divisions within the wider society may also operate to problematize and even undermine students' access to opportunities and resources within the school, as the cultural ecological theory indicates. In this way, the existing social structure and status quo are reproduced. This explanation therefore offers a more elaborate proposal for the way in which the social status gets reproduced. Unlike the social reproduction theory, it is specific in showing how aspects and processes in the school can work against certain groups. It also shows how aspects of the society – ideologies, antagonisms and conflicts – can be reproduced within the school. At the same time, like the cultural ecological theory, it includes students' and parents' psychological responses to explain why the low-status group achieves less than mainstream students. Stanton-Salazar calls for a special type of socialization for low-status students which includes the development of the discourses necessary for them to make the connections that will help them gain the social capital and cultural knowledge that is the basis for success.

A sixth explanation, which may be of special significance to post-colonial societies, highlights the curriculum and pedagogy of the school as the main reason that students of racially subordinated and/or working-class groups fail to do well in school in the United States. Educators and researchers who hold this perspective cite a hegemonic curriculum which is imposed by the dominant white society, and which ignores the cultural knowledge and experiences of subordinated groups. They also cite a pedagogy that is devoid of knowledge of and caring for working-class/racially subordinated students and their culture. They link the existence of such a curriculum and pedagogy to a racist society that devalues some racially subordinated and working-class groups. Those who hold this perspective blame the poor achievement of students from these racially subordinated and low socio-economic groups on a curriculum that is disconnected from the students' lives, and which in fact sometimes sends messages that students find unpalatable. They call for a culturally relevant curriculum and a culturally relevant pedagogy that enable students to make connections to their own culture and experiences.

The alternative curriculum would take different forms. Gordon, for example, calls for a curriculum that includes African and African American "cultural knowledge as expressed through the beliefs, values, perspectives, and worldview" of the group, as well as "popular culture . . . in terms of the literary arts, dance, media, theology, athletics, music, cinema and so forth" (1994, 64). Others, such as Ladson-Billings (1994, 2001), Villegas and Lucas (2002a, 2002b) and Foster (1995), call on teachers to infuse the curriculum with ideas and examples from the experiences and culture of their students so that students can make the connections that make learning meaningful. In so doing, these culturally responsive teachers validate their students' experiences and create connections that make learning meaningful. These educators argue that teachers and teacher candidates must begin to see the curriculum as flexible so that they can address students' concerns and be able to include in the curriculum topics with which the students identify, such as drug use and abuse, teenage sex and pregnancy, relationships with parents, relations between the sexes, popular culture, violence and any topics that are relevant to their lives and their communities. As Ladson-Billings (2001, 121) has argued, effective, culturally responsive teachers of urban students "know how to mine curriculum materials (that are limited) to stimulate students' thinking and their learning of critical skills".

In addition to such modifications to the curriculum, these educators also call for a different pedagogy that is culturally relevant and demonstrates knowledge of students and a desire on the part of teachers to relate in more human and caring ways with them, for teachers cannot rely only on knowledge of methods to connect with students – especially those from subordinated groups. Exhorting educators to go beyond the "methods fetish" or an over-reliance on and overvaluation of teaching methods as the basis for their ability to teach these students, educators who hold this view urge teachers to understand the political nature of education and to "take into consideration the socio-cultural realities that either limit or expand the possibilities to humanize education" (Bartolome 1994, 177). A pedagogy that is culturally responsive includes the following: teachers who have a high self-esteem and a high regard for their students; teachers who know about the lives of their students and believe all students can achieve; teachers who believe that all students have knowledge which teachers must identify, legitimize and build on; a humane and equitable relationship between teachers and students that extends beyond the classroom; teachers who demonstrate connectedness to learners and encourage the creation of learning communities and collaborative relationships; and teachers who have culturally relevant conceptions of knowledge, that is, knowledge is continuously re-created, and shared among teachers and students. This implies that knowledge is viewed critically and students have to learn the skills to do this critique (Ladson-Billings 1994, 2001; Villegas and Lucas 2002b). This type of curriculum and pedagogy are quite different from that which is found in most schools, including secondary schools, in Jamaica. It contrasts with what Connell (1985) has described as the competitive academic curriculum, in which the knowledge to be taught is derived from university-based disciplines, is organized hierarchically, and in which the pedagogy is basically transfer teaching. What the teacher knows about the subject matter is transferred to the pupil. Student learning is organized as appropriation of bits of knowledge, that is, they learn in parallel not in a joint or collaborative manner. Connell (1985) believes that this curriculum plays a critical role in structuring access to important resources in the society, but is not conducive to learning by students from poor and working-class groups.

Within the Caribbean, there have been calls to Caribbean educators to modify the curriculum so that students learn more about their own realities. Nettleford has appealed to Caribbean educators to find a way of "getting to the young through a learning process that links them organically to the realities of their own environment and to the potential of their creative capacities" (1993, 151). He quotes the Caribbean Union of Teachers, which in 1977 considered that the curriculum was elitist and geared for underachievement (150). In addition to a curriculum that is relevant and grounded in students' realities, Nettleford calls for the integration of cultural disciplines into the curriculum, echoing Gordon's (1994) call for cultural knowledge as expressed through the beliefs, values, perspectives, and worldviews, as well as popular culture such as the literary arts, dance, media, theology, athletics, music and cinema. Nettleford's and Gordon's critique recognizes the challenge facing a post-colonial education system, and the need to make radical changes in what students are expected to learn.

These six theoretical perspectives provide competing explanations for the educational achievement of students of working-class and racially subordinated groups in industrialized societies such as the United States and Canada.[1] Each of these six competing explanations includes concepts that can help us to conceptualize students' academic achievement. Each emphasizes one or more aspects of the environment in which the student is situated. The school, as a significant site for socialization and for developing the conditions for academic achievement, assumes different salience in each explanation. Four of the explanations highlight the importance of the social relationships that exist between adults and students within the school. In different ways, each of these four explanations point to the importance of good, trusting relationships between teachers and students. They also show that such respect is often based on the accord granted the social and racially subordinated group of the wider society to which the student belongs. The social support network theory and the cultural ecological theories underscore the need for relations that facilitate students' gaining social/cultural capital and know-how, and the ways in which support or exclusion can affect students. These two explanations also imply the importance of the empowerment of students through the acceptance of their socio-cultural background and the creation and negotiation of identities within the school.

The cultural reproduction theory points to the relationship that can be easily established between teachers and those students with the cultural capital valued by the school and can alert one to what can be missing for other students. The cultural production theory also alerts one to the responses that teachers may have to students' cultural expressions and the consequences of such responses. Some explanations are more helpful than others because of their comprehensiveness, or their focus on school-related processes, a fact which allows for research and for implementing change at the school level. The social support network highlights the processes that are critical to teacher-student interaction, learning and the precursors of learning. At the same time, aspects of the other explanations can provide useful insights into the causes of student academic achievement.

Note

1. Excluded from the explanations are the racial or cultural deficit explanations that denigrate the intelligence of some racially subordinated groups or people from poor backgrounds. I have also excluded theories that focus on communication processes, because they are more applicable to the early years of schooling. The communication process explanation of low achievement has been developed by socio-linguists who have studied culturally learned verbal and non-verbal communication styles of students who are taught by teachers who are ethnically or racially different. Teachers and students' expectations for behaviour are derived from their experience in different speech communities. These cultural differences between teachers and students result in teachers misinterpreting behaviours or speech acts, and to miscommunication (Erickson 1987). This theory does not explain successes where no modification is made in classroom communication patterns and has been criticized on the grounds that it ignores the wider socio-political context of education and schooling.

In addition to these theories, there are other explanations that focus on factors or variables each of which has statistically been shown to be related to student achievement. So, for example, Smith (2003), examining the academic performance and other input and contextual variables of 2,124 students of different socio-economic backgrounds, argued that what made the difference between the performance of students in the high and low socio-economic groups were attendance, motivation and attitudes to school. These differed by socio-economic group. Similarly, Darling-Hammond (1995, 2001) has cited structural explanations such as unequal funding, distribution of resources and unequal access to a quality curriculum within a school as some of the main reasons that some groups of students fail to do well in American schools. Structural explanations such as these and variables associated with socio-economic status such as ability to afford books and lunch will obviously affect groups of students.

Appendix 3   Interview Schedule for Teachers

Introductory Remarks

1. How long have you been a teacher? _____

2. How long have you been teaching at Hillview High School?

3. Can you remember what made you decide to become a teacher?

4. Did you teach 9X when they were in 8X?

5. If yes, was their behaviour the same as it has been this year?

6. Is there any way in which it is different from when they were in 8X?

7. When you think of the 9X class, what comes to mind?

8. In teaching your subject which is _____, what do you want to achieve with the students in 9X?

9. Why are these goals important to you?

10. When you are planning your lessons, what is uppermost in your mind? (Probe) What [do] you pay most attention to in planning for your lessons?

11. Is there a lesson plan format for this school?

12. How do you take the students' needs into account in your planning or in your teaching?

13. How do you assess how well you are doing as a teacher? (Probe) How do you know how well you are doing as a teacher with this class?

14. I have noticed that students are at different levels in that class. How do you deal with that?

15. What curriculum guide do you use?

16. Do you have any concerns about the curriculum in your subject? (Probe) For example, difficulty level for students, relevance to students, etc.

17. What do you do if you realize that a particular lesson you are teaching is not working? (Probe) For example, the students do not show any interest or have difficulty understanding.

18. What do you pay attention to if you want to know if they understand?

19. What do you think is the most important attribute of a good teacher?

20. What support do you get from the administration of the school for your teaching?

21. With the difficulties that you and other teachers face, what keeps you in teaching?

Thank you

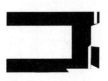

Appendix 4   Interview Schedule for Students' Focus Groups

Introductory Remarks

A. The School

1. What do you like best about this school?
2. And what do you not like about Hillview High?
3. If you could change something about your school, what would you change?
4. Think back to the day you first started at Hillview High. How have you changed as a person since you started coming to this school?

B. The Curriculum

5. Which subject do you like the most?
6. Why do you like this subject? (Let each student answer in turn.)

7. So how about the other subjects that you don't like. What is it about these other subjects that make you not like them? (There are now about ten subjects on your timetable.)

8. Do you think you are getting a good education at Hillview High?

9. Do you think that what you are learning at this school will help you to realize your dreams or help you later in life?

10. If yes, what are some of the things that you are learning now that will help you in later life?

11. Do you feel that much of what you are learning is relevant to your life or is important?

C. Teachers and Teaching

12. What about your teachers? How do you feel about them?

13. Do you find your teachers helpful? Which ones are helpful?

14. Who is your favourite teacher? Why?

15. What do you look for in a teacher? What do you expect from your teachers? (*or*) If you could think of an ideal teacher how would you describe him or her?

16. Let us talk a bit about teaching. Do you find the teachers interesting? Are their classes interesting?

17. Tell me what an interesting class is like. What are some of the things that make a lesson really good or interesting?

18. If you were to teach your classes for a week, what kinds of things would you do or let your students do?

19. What are some of the things that you like teachers to do when they are teaching you?

20. Do you think that your teachers explain things well for you to understand?

21. What happens when you do not understand something in class?
(Probe) Do you ask the teacher questions or ask for explanations?
(Probe) Do you ever get additional time with a teacher to explain something?

22. What happens when the grades are not good? What do you do? What does the teacher do?

23. Do you have many boring classes? What do you do when the class is boring?

24. I notice that the teacher often calls one of the students to read aloud in class. Do you like to do this? Why?

25. How do you deal with the noise in your class? Does it disturb you at all? (Probe) Are you able to learn well when there is so much noise?

26. If you could make suggestions on how we could improve teaching at Hillside, what recommendations would you make?

D. Classroom Culture/Climate

27. Tell me about your classroom. Do you think that you get a lot of work done in this class?

28. I notice that some students sometimes skull classes. Why is that?

28a. What happens when you skull classes and teachers find out? Do teachers always find out?

29. Do you ever feel that you waste time in class?

E. Academic Self-Concept/Gender

30. Are there many bright students in your class?

Which students in 9X are the bright students in your class?

31. Do you think of yourself as a bright student?
(Probe) Are you good at your school work?

32. What makes a boy popular? Who are the popular boys in 9X?

33. What makes a girl popular? Who are the popular girls in your class?

34. What do you think of boys who are studious, pay attention and work hard at their school work?
(Probe) Is it okay for a boy to be studious?

35. What do you think of girls who are studious, pay attention and work hard at their school work?
(Probe) Is it okay for a girl to be studious

36. Do you behave or talk differently when boys/ girls are in the conversation? What is different? Why?

37. Do you think that the teachers are easier on the girls than the boys? Why?

Appendix 5   Interview Questions for the Vice-Principal

Introduction

Mrs ————, thanks for agreeing to see me. This is not an interview in the formal sense. I would like to follow up on some issues that have come up during the research. Just to clarify or to get some additional information.

1. First, extra-curricular activities. These are activities that are scheduled after school. What are these activities?

    Is there any rule that states that students must participate?

    What incentives are offered for students to participate, or any sanctions when they do not?

2. How does the school address the all-round development of the students? What are the specific ways in which it does this?

3. To what extent are parents involved in the running of the school?
   In what ways are they involved at all in the school, apart from Parent-Teacher Association meetings?

4. What connections does the school have to the community. Is there anything that you can call school-community relationship?

5. A totally different question has to do with teacher planning. Teachers are given a teachers' diary which, I understand, records lesson plans.

   What else are teachers to do with this book?

   Is it used for any other purposes?

   Is it monitored? And if so, by whom?

6. What is the role of the grade supervisor?

7. What is the role of the head of department?

8. What kind of supervision do teachers get?

9. What is the total number of staff at Hillview High?

10. Curriculum for grade 9 – is it CXC or ROSE?

11. What are the Options A, B, C, D at grade 10?

12. Now to another matter. The ——— teacher left at the end of December last year. May I ask what were the circumstances surrounding his leaving?

13. Finally, did we talk about this before, the GSAT scores for last year's 9X? Is it possible to take a look at these?

Thank you.

Appendix 6   Interview with Guidance Counsellors

1. To begin – how long have you been a guidance counsellor?

2. Why did you become a guidance counsellor?

3. And do you also teach?

4. With respect to 9X, did you teach them last year?

5. Have they changed, at all, from last year to this year?
   (Probe for clarification.)

6. What do you do in the Personal Development classes?

7. On what occasions do you see students as individuals?

8. On what occasions do you see parents? What causes you to have to call in parents?

9. Do parents ever call you? And if so what do they call about?

10. How many students would be in that category that need additional counselling?

11. And when they are referred by the form teacher, what kind of behaviour would the form teacher see?

12. Are the issues easily resolved?

13. Do you see any gender differences in these issues?

14. What typical issues do the girls face?

15. What typical issues do the boys face?

16. What are the main concerns that you have about the students at this school?

17. Do you get a chance to talk with the teachers in the school?

18. I have been talking to the students, and they all have a complaint about the way they are talked to and the relationship they have with adults.

19. Have you had a chance to talk to parents as a group?

20. What are the main issues that are on students' minds at this school?

21. From your involvement with the students, what percentage would have issues like that?

22. What additional resources would you like to have to do a really good job of what you are doing?

23. Do you intend to stay in this profession given all the challenges that you face?

Thank you very much.

Appendix 7   Student Questionnaire
Grade 10 Students
(Grade 9X, 2003–2004)

I am interested in knowing what you think about life in school, your life outside of school and your plans for the future. Please complete the items below. *In each of the sections below, you are asked to complete the blanks or tick the appropriate response.* Your responses will be held in strict confidence. Thank you very much for your cooperation.

The questions in this section ask for basic information about yourself and your family.

1. How old are you?

2. What class are you in now? (September 2004)

3. Are you male or female?
   ( ) Male
   ( ) Female

4. Who is responsible for you at home? (With whom do you live at home?)
   ( ) Your mother only

( ) Your father only
( ) Your mother and father
( ) Your mother and stepfather
( ) Your father and stepmother
( ) Your grandmother or grandfather
( ) Your guardian (aunt, uncle, brother, sister, cousin)
( ) Other person?

5. What does your father or male guardian do for a living?

6. What does you mother or female guardian do for a living?

7. My parent(s)/guardian(s) always insist that I do my homework
( ) Yes
( ) No

8. On a typical weekend or weekday after school, please describe what you do at home.

The questions in this section are about life at school.

9. Do you think you are doing well at school?
( ) Yes – Go to item 10
( ) No – Go to item 11

10. What is the main reason why you are doing well at school?
( ) I study hard
( ) I do my homework
( ) I am a bright student
( ) Teachers teach well
( ) Other reason?

11. What is the main reason why you are not doing well at school?
( ) I don't study enough/I don't have enough time to study
( ) Too many distractions outside of school
( ) I am not a bright student
( ) Teachers don't teach well
( ) Other reason?

12. How can the school help you to improve your grades at school?
    ( ) Offer make-up classes after school or on weekends
    ( ) Assign more homework
    ( ) Teachers teach better
    ( ) Have special tutoring in the subject
    ( ) Other suggestion?

13. What subject(s) would you like to do at school but is not offered?

14. I sometimes feel I don't belong in school.
    ( ) Strongly agree
    ( ) Agree
    ( ) Undecided
    ( ) Disagree
    ( ) Strongly disagree

15. I like being in school most of the time.
    ( ) Strongly agree
    ( ) Agree
    ( ) Undecided
    ( ) Disagree
    ( ) Strongly disagree

16. The teachers make their classes interesting most of the time.
    ( ) Strongly agree
    ( ) Agree
    ( ) Undecided
    ( ) Disagree
    ( ) Strongly disagree

The questions in this section are about how you see yourself in the future.

17. What job or career would you like to have when you grow up?

18. How do you see your life in ten years' time?

19. What does being a man mean to you?

20. What does being a woman mean to you?

The questions in this section relate to how you feel about yourself.

21. I worry about the present and the future.
    ( ) All the time
    ( ) Most of the time
    ( ) Sometimes
    ( ) Now and then
    ( ) Never – go to item 23

22. If you worry about the present and the future, what do you worry about?
    ( ) Being able to stay in school
    ( ) Passing my CXC exams
    ( ) Being able to go on to study after CXC
    ( ) Getting a job when I am older
    ( ) Violence in my community
    ( ) Physical or sexual abuse
    ( ) Parents/guardians leaving
    ( ) Parents/ guardians being hurt
    ( ) Getting pregnant or getting a girl pregnant
    ( ) Discrimination (on the basis of colour, gender, etc.)
    ( ) Other

23. What is the most important thing in your life at the moment?

24. I feel good about myself
    ( ) All the time
    ( ) Most of the time
    ( ) Sometimes
    ( ) Now and then
    ( ) Never

Thank you very much for taking the time to complete this questionnaire. Please return this questionnaire in the envelope provided to the researcher.

References

Ancess, J. 2004. "Snapshots of Meaning Making in Classrooms". *Educational Leadership* 62, no. 1 (September): 36–40.

Anderson, G. 1989. "Critical Ethnography in Education: Origins, Current Status, and New Directions". *Review of Educational Research* 59, no. 3: 249–70.

Anyon, J. 1995. "Race, Social Class and Educational Reform in an Inner City School". *Teachers College Record* 97, no. 1: 69–94.

Apple, M. 1972. *Education and Power*. Boston: Routledge and Kegan Paul.

——. 1996. "Power, Meaning and Identity: Critical Sociology of Education in the United States". *British Journal of Sociology of Education* 17, no. 2: 125–44.

Austin, D. 1984. *Urban Life in Kingston, Jamaica: The Culture and Class Ideology of Two Neighborhoods*. New York: Gordon and Breach Science Publishers.

Austin-Broos, D. 2001. "Race/Class: Jamaica's Discourse of Heritable Identity". In *Caribbean Sociology: Introductory Readings*, ed. C. Barrow and R. Reddock. Kingston: Ian Randle.

Barrow, C. 2001. *Children's Rights, Caribbean Realities*. Kingston: Ian Randle.

Bartolome, L. 1994. "Beyond the Methods Fetish: Toward a Humanizing Pedagogy". *Harvard Educational Review* 64, no. 2: 173–94.

Bearman, P., J. Jones and J. Udry. 1997. *Reducing the Risk: Connections That Make a Difference in the Lives of Youth*. Minneapolis: University of Minnesota Press.

Blythe, T., and Associates. 1998. *The Teaching for Understanding Guide.* San Francisco: Jossey-Bass.

Bogdan, R., and S. Biklen. 1998. *Qualitative Research Methods for Education.* Boston: Allyn and Bacon.

Bourdieu, P. 1977. "Cultural Reproduction and Social Reproduction". In *Power and Ideology in Education,* ed. J. Karabel and A. Halsey. New York: Oxford University Press.

Bourdieu, P., and J.C. Passeron. 1977. *Reproduction in Education, Society and Culture.* London: Sage.

Bowles, H., and H. Gintis. 1976. *Schooling in Capitalist America.* New York: Basic Books.

Bronfenbrenner, U. 1995. "Ecology of the Family as a Context for Human Development". *Developmental Psychology* 22: 723–42.

Brown, B., and W. Theobald. 1998. "Learning Contexts beyond the Classroom: Extra-Curricular Activities, Community Organizations, and Peer Groups". In *The Adolescent Years: Social Influences and Adolescent Challenges,* Ninety-seventh Yearbook of the National Society for the Study of Education, ed. K. Borman and B. Schneider. Chicago: University of Chicago Press.

Brown, D. 1994. *Reassessing and Rationalizing Resources for Greater Results: A Tracer Study of Graduates of Jamaican Secondary Schools.* Kingston: Education Research Centre, University of the West Indies.

Brown, J. 2001. "Parental Resistance to Child Rights in Jamaica". In *Children's Rights, Caribbean Realities,* ed. C. Barrow. Kingston: Ian Randle.

Bryan, P. 2000a. *Inside Out and Outside In: Factors in the Creation of Contemporary Jamaica.* Kingston: Grace, Kennedy Foundation.

———. 2000b. *The Jamaican People 1880–1902: Race, Class and Social Control.* Kingston: University of the West Indies Press.

Chevannes, B. 1993. "Sexual Behaviour of Jamaicans: A Literature Review". *Social and Economic Studies* 42: 1–45.

Chuck, D. 2004. "Failing Grades in Education". *Gleaner.* 17 November.

Clarke, A. 1980. *Growing Up Stupid under the Union Jack.* Toronto: Vintage.

Coleman, J. 1987. "Families and Schools". *Educational Researcher* 16, no. 6: 32–38.

Connell, R.W. 1985. *Teachers Work.* Sydney: George Unwin.

———. 1987. *Gender and Power.* Stanford: Stanford University Press.

———. 1993. *Schools and Social Justice.* Philadelphia: Temple University Press.

———. 1994. "Poverty and Education". *Harvard Educational Review* 64, no. 2: 125–49.

Connell, R.W., D.J. Ashenden, S. Kessler and G.W. Dowsett. 1982. *Making the Difference: Schools, Families and Social Divisions.* St Leonards, New South Wales, Australia: Allen and Unwin.

References

Crawford-Brown, C. 1999. *Who Will Save Our Children? The Plight of the Jamaican Child in the 1990s.* Kingston: Canoe Press.

Cummins, J. 1997. "Minority Status and Schooling in Canada". *Anthropology and Education Quarterly* 28, no. 3: 411–30.

Darling-Hammond, L. 1995. "Inequality and Access to Knowledge". In *Handbook of Research on Multi-Cultural Education,* ed. J. Banks and C. Banks. New York: Macmillan.

————. 1999. "Investing in Teaching as the Learning Profession: Policy Problems and Prospects". In *Teaching as the Learning Profession,* ed. L. Darling-Hammond and G. Sykes. San Francisco: Jossey-Bass.

————. 2000. "Teacher Quality and Student Achievement: A Review of State Policy Evidence". *Education Policy Analysis Archives* 8, no. 1: 1–30.

Davidson, A. 1996. *Making and Molding Identity in Schools: Student Narratives on Race, Gender, and Academic Engagement.* Albany: State University of New York Press.

Deschenes, S., L. Cuban and D. Tyack. 2001. "Mismatch: Historical Perspectives on Schools and Students Who Don't Fit Them". *Teachers College Record* 103, no. 4: 525–47.

Dei, G., J. Mazzuca, E. McIsaac and J. Zine. 1997. *Reconstructing Drop-outs: A Critical Ethnography of the Dynamics of Black Students' Disengagement from School.* Toronto: University of Toronto Press.

Denzin, N., and Y. Lincoln. 2000. "Introduction: The Discipline and Practice of Qualitative Research". In *Handbook of Qualitative Research,* 2nd ed., ed. N. Denzin and Y. Lincoln. Thousand Oaks, CA: Sage.

Doyle, W. 1983. "Academic Work". *Review of Educational Research* 53, no. 2: 159–99.

————. 1992. "Curriculum and Pedagogy". In *Handbook of Research on Curriculum,* ed. P.W. Jackson. New York: Macmillan.

Eggleston, E., J. Jackson and K. Hunter. 1999. "Sexual Attitudes and Behaviour among Young Adolescents in Jamaica". *International Family Planning Perspectives* 25, no. 2: 78–84.

Ennis C., and T. McCauley. 2002. "Creating Urban Classroom Communities Worthy of Trust". *Journal of Curriculum Studies* 34, no. 2: 149–72.

Erickson, F. 1986. "Qualitative Methods in Research on Teaching". In *Handbook of Research on Teaching,* 3rd ed., ed. M. Wittrock. New York: Macmillan.

————. 1987. "Transformation and School Success: The Politics and Culture of Educational Achievement". *Anthropology and Education Quarterly* 18: 335–56.

Evans, H. 1997. *Research on Secondary Education in Jamaica.* Kingston: Faculty of Education, University of the West Indies.

————. 1998. *Gender and Achievement in Secondary Education in Jamaica.* Kingston: Planning Institute of Jamaica.

————. 1999. "Streaming and Its Effects on Boys and Girls in Secondary Schools in Jamaica". *Journal of Education and Development in the Caribbean* 3, no. 1: 45–60.

————. 2001. *Inside Jamaican Schools.* Kingston: University of the West Indies Press.

Feiman-Nemser, S., and J. Remillard. 1995. "Perspectives on Learning to Teach". In *The Teacher Educator's Handbook,* ed. F. Murray. San Francisco: Jossey-Bass.

Feldman, S., and G. Elliott. 1993. *At the Threshold: The Developing Adolescent.* Cambridge: Harvard University Press.

Ferguson, A. 2000. *Bad Boys: Public Schools in the Making of Black Masculinity.* Ann Arbor: University of Michigan Press.

Fine, M. 1991. *Framing Dropouts: Notes on the Politics of an Urban Public High School.* New York: State University of New York Press.

Fordham, S. 1988. "Racelessness as a Factor in Black Students' Success: Pragmatic Strategy or Pyrrhic Victory". *Harvard Educational Review* 58, no. 1: 54–84.

Foster, M. 1995. "African-American Teachers and Culturally Relevant Pedagogy". In *Handbook of Research on Multi-Cultural Education,* ed. J. Banks and C. Banks. New York: Macmillan.

Giddens, A. 1979. *Central Problems in Social Theory: Action, Structure and Contradiction in Social Analysis.* Berkeley and Los Angeles: University of California Press.

Gilligan, C. 1982. *In a Different Voice.* Cambridge: Harvard University Press.

Gilligan, C., and J. Taylor. 2004. *Between Voice and Silence: Women and Girls, Race and Relationships.*

Giroux, H. 1996. *Fugitive Cultures: Race, Violence and Youth.* New York: Routledge.

Goodlad J., C. Mantle-Bromley and S.J. Goodlad. 2004. *Education for Everyone: Agenda for Education in a Democracy.* San Francisco: Jossey-Bass.

Gordon, B. 1994. "African American Cultural Knowledge and Liberatory Education: Dilemmas, Problems, and Potentials in Postmodern American Society". In *Too Much Schooling, too Little Education: A Paradox in Black Life in White Societies,* ed. M. Shujaa. Trenton, NJ: Africa World Press.

Gordon, D. 1991. "Access to High School Education in Postwar Jamaica". In *Education and Society in the Commonwealth Caribbean,* ed. E. Miller. Kingston: Institute of Social and Economic Research.

Great Britain. Board of Education. 1901. *Education Systems of the Chief Colonies of the British Empire.* Board of Education Report.

Griffin, C. 1993. *Representations of Youth: The Study of Youth and Adolescence in Britain and America.* Oxford: Polity Press.

Gurian, M., and K. Stevens. 2004. "With Boys and Girls in Mind". *Educational Leadership* 62, no. 3 (November): 21–26.

Hamilton, M. 1991. "A Review of Educational Research in Jamaica". In *Education and Society in the Commonwealth Caribbean*, ed. E. Miller. Kingston: Institute of Social and Economic Research.

Hammersley, M., and P. Atkinson. 1993. *Ethnography: Principles in Practice.* London: Routledge.

hooks, b. 2000. *Where We Stand: Class Matters.* New York: Routledge.

Jackson, A. 1997. "Adapting Educational Systems to Young Adolescents and New Conditions". In *Preparing Adolescents for the Twenty-first Century*, ed. R. Takanishi and D. Hamburg. Cambridge: Cambridge University Press.

James, C.L.R. 1963. *Beyond a Boundary.* London: Hutchinson.

Jones, A. 1989. "The Cultural Production of Classroom Practice". *British Journal of Sociology of Education* 10, no. 1: 19–31.

Karabel, J., and A.H. Halsey, eds. 1977. *Power and Ideology in Education.* Oxford: Oxford University Press.

Keith, S. 1976. "Socialization in the Jamaican Primary School: A Study of Teacher Evaluation and Student Participation". In *Sociology of Education: A Caribbean Reader*, ed. P. Figueroa and G. Persaud. London: Oxford University Press.

Kelly, H. 2003. "Implementing the ROSE Language Arts Curriculum in Three Junior High Schools". MA thesis, University of the West Indies, Mona.

Kempadoo, K. 2003. "Sexuality in the Caribbean: Theory and Research (with an Emphasis on the Anglophone Caribbean)". *Social and Economic Studies* 52, no. 3: 59–88.

King, R. 1998. "Educational Inequality in Jamaica: The Need for Reform". In *Institute of Education Annual*, ed. R. King. Kingston: Institute of Education, University of the West Indies.

———. 1999. "Education in the British Caribbean: The Legacy of the Nineteenth Century". In *Educational Reform in the Commonwealth Caribbean*, ed. E. Miller. Washington, DC: Organization of American States Publications.

Ladson-Billings, G. 1990. "Culturally Relevant Teaching". *Teachers College Record* 155: 20–25.

———. 1994. *The Dream Keepers: Successful Teachers of African American Children.* San Francisco: Jossey-Bass.

———. 2001. *Crossing over to Canaan: The Journey of New Teachers in Diverse Classrooms.* San Francisco: Jossey-Bass.

Leo-Rhynie, E. 1997. "Class, Race and Gender Issues in Child Rearing in the Caribbean". In *Caribbean Families: Diversity among Ethnic Groups*, ed. J. Roopnarine and J. Brown. Greenwich, CT: Ablex.

Levinson, B., D. Foley and D. Holland. 1996. *The Cultural Production of the Educated Person: Critical Ethnographies of Schooling and Local Practice.* Albany: State University of New York Press.

McLaren, P. 1989. *Life in Schools.* New York: Longman.

McNeil, L. 1986. *Contradictions of Control: School Structure and School Knowledge.* New York: Routledge and Kegan Paul.

Mehan, H. 1992. "Understanding Inequality in Schools: The Contribution of Interpretive Studies". *Sociology of Education* 65 (January): 1–20.

Metz, M. 1993. "Teachers' Ultimate Dependence on Their Students". In *Teacher Work: Individuals, Colleagues and Contexts,* ed. J. Little and M. McLaughlin. New York: Teachers College Press.

Miller, E. 1989. "Educational Development in Independent Jamaica". In *Jamaica in Independence: Essays on the Early Years,* ed. R. Nettleford. Kingston: Heinemann.

Ministry of Education, Youth and Culture. 2003. *Corporate Plan 2003–2006.* Kingston: Ministry of Education, Youth and Culture.

Nespor, J. 1987. "Academic Tasks in a High School English Class". *Curriculum Inquiry.* 17, no. 2: 203–28.

Nettleford, R. 1993. *Inward Stretch, Outward Reach: A Voice from the Caribbean.* London: Macmillan.

Newman, F. 1998. "Institutional and Social Supports for Youth". In *The Adolescent Years: Social Influences and Adolescent Challenges,* Ninety-seventh Yearbook of the National Society for the Study of Education, ed. K. Borman and B. Schneider. Chicago: University of Chicago Press.

Noddings, N. 2002. *Educating Moral People: A Caring Alternative to Character Education.* New York: Teachers College Press.

Oakes, J. 1985. *Keeping Track: How Schools Structure Inequality.* New Haven: Yale University Press.

———. 1992. "Can Tracking Research Inform Practice? Technical, Normative, and Political Considerations". *Educational Researcher* 21, no. 4: 12–22.

Ogbu, J. 1974. *The Next Generation: an Ethnography of an Urban Neighborhood.* New York: Academic Press.

———. 1999. "Beyond Language: Ebonics, Proper English, and Identity in a Black-American Speech Community". *American Educational Research Journal* 36, no. 2: 147–84.

Perkins, D. 2004. "Knowledge Alive". *Educational Leadership* 62, no. 1 (September): 14–19.

Phillips, A. 1973. *Adolescence in Jamaica.* Kingston: Jamaica Publishing House.

Proweller, A. 1998. *Constructing Female Identities: Meaning Making in an Upper Middle Class Youth Culture.* Albany: State University of New York Press.

Roopnarine, J. 2004. "African American and African Caribbean Fathers: Level, Quality, and Meaning of Involvement". In *The Role of the Father in Child Development*, 4th ed., ed. M. Lamb. New York: Wiley.

Rumberger, R. 1987. "High School Dropouts: A Review of Issues and Evidence". *Review of Educational Research* 57, no. 2: 101–21.

Santrock, J. 2004. *Adolescence*, 9th ed. New York: McGraw-Hill.

Schaps, E., V. Battistich and D. Solomon. 1997. "School as a Caring Community: A Key to Character Education", in *The Construction of Children's Character*, Ninety-sixth Yearbook of the National Society for the Study of Education, ed. A. Molnar. Chicago: University of Chicago Press.

Senior, O. 1991. *Working Miracles: Women's Lives in the English-Speaking Caribbean.* Bloomington: Indiana University Press.

———. 2003. *Encyclopedia of Jamaican Heritage.* Kingston: Twin Guinep.

Sewell, T. 1997. *Black Masculinities and Schooling: How Black Boys Survive Modern Schooling.* Stoke-on-Trent, UK: Trentham Books.

Sherlock, P., and H. Bennett. 1998. *The Story of the Jamaican People.* Kingston: Ian Randle.

Shulman, L. 1986. "Those Who Understand, Teach: Knowledge Growth in a Profession". *Educational Researcher* 15, no. 2: 4–114.

Sistren, with Honor Ford Smith. 1986. *Lionheart Gal: Life Stories of Jamaican Women.* London: Women's Press.

Slavin, R. 1990. "Achievement Effects of Ability Grouping in Secondary Schools: A Best Evidence Synthesis". *Review of Educational Research* 60, no. 3: 471–99.

Smith, E. 2003. "Understanding Underachievement: An Investigation into the Differential Attainment of Secondary School Pupils". *British Journal of Sociology of Education* 24, no. 5: 575–85.

Solomon, P. 1992. *Black Resistance in High School: Forging a Separatist Culture.* Albany: State University of New York Press.

Stake, R. 2000. "Case Studies". In *Handbook of Qualitative Research*, ed. N. Denzin and Y. Lincoln. 2nd ed. Thousand Oaks, CA: Sage.

Stanton-Salazar, R. 1997. "A Social Capital Framework for Understanding the Socialization of Racial Minority Children and Youth". *Harvard Education Review* 67, no. 1: 1–40.

Statistical Institute of Jamaica (STATIN). 1991. *Jamaica Standard Occupational Classification.* Kingston: STATIN.

———. 1998. *Survey of Living Conditions 1998.* Kingston: STATIN.

———. 2002a. *Demographic Statistics, 2002.* Kingston: STATIN.

———. 2002b. *Jamaica Survey of Living Conditions, 2002.* Kingston: STATIN.

Swanson, D., M. Spencer and A. Petersen. 1998. "Identity Formation in Adolescence". In *The Adolescent Years: Social Influences and Adolescent Challenges,* Ninety-seventh Yearbook of the National Society for the Study of Education, ed. K. Borman and B. Schneider. Chicago: University of Chicago Press.

Talbert, J., M. McLaughlin and B. Rowan. 1993. "Understanding Context Effects on Secondary Teaching". *Teachers College Record* 95, no. 1: 45–68.

Tharp, R., P. Estrada, S. Dalton and L. Yamauchi. 2000. *Teaching Transformed: Achieving Excellence, Fairness, Inclusion and Harmony.* Boulder: Westview.

Thompson, H. 2000. *Rural Gumption: A Chronicle of the Life Struggles and Successes of a Determined Dreamer.* Kingston: Dikah Publishers.

Thompson, R. 2003. "CXC Results: Total Disaster". *Gleaner.* 3 October.

Turner, T. 1987. "The Socialization Intent in Colonial Jamaican Education, 1967–1911". *Caribbean Journal of Education* 14, nos. 1–2: 54–87.

Villegas, A., and T. Lucas. 2002a. "Preparing Culturally Responsive Teachers: Rethinking the Curriculum". *Journal of Teacher Education* 53, no. 1: 20–32.

———. 2002b. *Educating Culturally Responsive Teachers: A Coherent Approach.* Albany: State University of New York Press.

Warren Little, Judith. 1999. "Organizing Schools for Teacher Learning". In *Teaching as the Learning Profession,* ed. L. Darling-Hammond and G. Sykes. San Francisco: Jossey-Bass.

West, C. 1999. "The Postmodern Crisis of the Black Intellectuals". In *Cultural Studies,* ed. L. Grossberg, C. Nelson and P. Treichler. London: Routledge.

West Indian Commission. 1992. *Time for Action: A Report of the West Indian Commmision.* Black Rock, Barbados: West Indian Commission.

Willis, P. 1977. *Learning to Labour.* Farnborough: Saxon House.

World Bank. 2003. *Caribbean Youth Development: Issues and Policy Directions.* Washington, DC: World Bank Publications.

Youdell, D. 2003. "Identity Traps or How Black Students Fail: The Interactions between Biographical, Sub-Cultural, and Learner Identities". *British Journal of Sociology of Education* 24, no. 1: 3–20.

Index